FOREWORD

Since its original publication this long-popular work has passed through twenty editions in various forms. The original type having been worn out while the author was yet living, he completely reworked the book and it was republished from new type in 1945.

In response to repeated demand for a smaller and less expensive edition for distribution and for use in Sunday schools, this new abridged edition has been prepared. The contents of this edition involve no change in fundamentals. The abridgment has been done with great care by a minister who served as the associate to the author during his last pastorate. The actual work was undertaken with the co-operation of the author's widow, and this edition has her approval.

Much of the space reduction was accomplished through reducing the number of Bible references printed in full, and through the use of footnotes indicating where fuller discussions of some subjects may be found. For the convenience of those familiar with the complete work, the major division headings and chapter titles have been preserved throughout as in previous editions.

If the author were yet living he might well send out this edition with words similar to those he used in earlier editions, "Praying that God will in the future bless this work to the good of his cause as he has in past years, I present this twenty-first and abridged edition to the public."

The Publishers

CONTENTS

PRELIMINARY

CONCERNING DIVINE LAW AND THE KINGDOM
OF GOD

CONCERNING THE DOCTRINE OF FINAL THINGS

PRELIMINARY

THE DIVINE AUTHORITY OF THE SCRIPTURES
Special Evidences of Divine Authorship

The truth of the Bible is apparent from its nature, but its authority is dependent altogether upon its source. The more carefully and reverentially we study the sacred Scriptures, the more deeply are we impressed with the fact that they have proceeded from one source. True, the Bible consists of many books, penned by various writers during a period of fifteen hundred years, but there exists throughout a grand unity and harmony that suggest divine inspiration. The writers themselves did not claim to be the authors of the messages they delivered, but, as the Apostle Peter affirms, they "spake as they were moved by the Holy Ghost" (II Pet. 1:21). Their writings encompass a variety of subjects—the origin of things, history, prophecy, biography, law and government, moral philosophy, ethics, theology, and poetry; still there exists a remarkable harmony of sentiment and teaching such as can be found in no other collection of books.

The revelation that the Scriptures make of the one true and living God testifies to its source. While the idea of a Supreme Being is universal, his nature and his relations with men are necessarily subjects of revelation. The history of all heathenism fails to disclose in one single instance the conception of a pure, holy God kindly disposed toward the human race. On the other hand, the mythologies of heathen nations abound with the most shocking and disgusting details of the actions of the gods whom they worship. The history of the Hebrew people given in the Bible shows that they, like other nations, were prone to evil of the deepest and blackest type. Whence, then, did they derive the idea of a God of holiness, a God who was opposed to all their evils, and yet gracious and full of mercy? When even Athens was devoting thousands of her choicest women to the lustful service of Venus; when Corinth, accord-

ing to Strabo, had a thousand sacred prostitutes in one temple
—who, I ask, taught the Israelites the principle of holiness and
gave them such exalted moral conceptions of God?

Many of the special messengers of God by whom the Bible
was written were given the power of performing miracles, by
which their inspiration was attested and their messages made
authoritative; but the "more sure word of prophecy" (II Pet.
1:19) furnishes the greatest external proof of its inspiration.
To this, more than to anything else, Christ and the Apostles
made their constant appeal. Matthew, narrating the deeds of
the Savior, gives us the standing phrase, "that it might be fulfilled which was spoken by the prophet"; Peter affirms, in
words unmistakable, that "holy men of God spake as they were
moved by the Holy Ghost" (vs. 21). From such facts as these
Paul adduces his conclusion relative to the authority of the
Bible, in these words: "All scripture is given by inspiration of
God, and is profitable for doctrine, for reproof, for correction,
for instruction in righteousness" (II Tim. 3:16).

The marvelous prophecy which Christ made concerning the
destruction of Jerusalem and the ruin and dispersal of the Jews
has been fulfilled with such unquestionable exactness that the
boldest infidels dare not deny the agreement.

The fifty-third chapter of Isaiah describes Christ's crucifixion and atonement work with such accuracy of detail that
the inspiration of the prophet is assured.

Other Proofs of Divine Authorship

There are many other proofs of the divine authorship of
the Bible, but I shall refer to only a few.

While the Bible speaks of the lowest forms of sin in the
plainest language, they are named only to be condemned. No
unprejudiced person can read the sacred pages without realizing that the Book stands for all that is good and is forever
opposed to all that is evil. It pronounces the last word on moral
character. The mind of man has never conceived anything so
noble, so elevating, so inspiring, so grand, as the Sermon on
the Mount. Search through all the religions of the ages, glean
out every choice moral precept and delineation of human character and conduct, place the findings together in one collection,

and they will bear no real comparison with the divine beauty and the infinite wisdom here expressed by the Christ of the Bible. Here is given the spiritual essence of the Law and the Prophets. Here truth is pressed home to the human soul, and character and conduct are defined by the secret springs and motives of the heart. Here all pride, hypocrisy, and self-seeking stand condemned; while all the finer virtues of which the soul is capable find free expression and infinite encouragement in the incomparable Beatitudes. Here a restraining influence is brought to bear upon wicked men by the solemn assertion of a future state of punishment in hell, while the righteous are assured of a great reward in heaven.

Another beautiful feature of God's Word *is its simplicity.* Though it contains the choicest wisdom of the ages, still it meets the wants and requirements of the unlearned and illiterate. "The wayfaring men, though fools, shall not err therein" (Isa. 35:8). The way of salvation, though straight and narrow, is not hidden, and there is nothing to hinder any seeking soul from coming in contact with its Maker. Blessed thought!

One of the clearest proofs that the Bible is the Word of God is the fact that *it now transforms human character* and accomplishes the regeneration of society. The promises of salvation and deliverance contained in its pages are, in millions of instances, proved to be living realities. The words of men have never accomplished such results as these. The Bible bears on its face the stamp of divine inspiration, and through belief in its message the work of God is performed in the world. Millions of redeemed men and women have given their lives in its defense, and today it is loved and reverenced by the worthy ones of earth.

The Bible Claims Divine Authorship

Furthermore, the Bible claims divine inspiration. "Hear the word of the Lord," cries Isaiah; "Give ear, O earth: for the Lord hath spoken" (1:2). "The Lord said unto me" are the words of Jeremiah (1:7). "The word of the Lord came expressly unto Ezekiel" (1:3). "Holy men of God spake as they were moved by the Holy Ghost" (II Pet. 1:21). (See also John 5:39, 46; Luke 16:31; Heb. 10:7; II Pet. 1:19.)

The Apostles themselves were specially inspired by the Spirit. (See Matt. 10:19-20; I Thess. 2:13; I Cor. 14:37; II Pet. 3:15-16; II Tim. 3:16.)

The Bible emerges from every legitimate test, external and internal, with glories undimmed, bearing every evidence that its message is indeed the word of God; hence its absolute authority is forever settled.

CONCERNING GOD

Chapter 1

THE DOCTRINE OF GOD

By the term "God" we mean the perfect, intelligent, conscious, moral Being existing from eternity, the Cause of all created things. This idea seems so natural that the majority of men accept it as self-evident truth without hesitating to give it any particular thought.

The writers of the Scriptures do not argue the existence of God. The first chapter of the Bible opens with the words, "In the beginning God," and everywhere his being is assumed. The Scriptures do contain the revelation that he has made of his own nature and attributes. These attributes are so well understood and so generally acknowledged that I shall merely refer to them, not giving the multitude of texts by which they are set forth in the Scriptures.

His Attributes

1. *Self-existence.* "The Father hath life in himself" (John 5:26). "For with thee is the fountain of life" (Ps. 36:9). He is underived and inexhaustible.

2. *Eternity.* "Before the mountains were brought forth, or ever thou hadst formed the earth and the world, even from everlasting to everlasting, thou art God" (Ps. 90:2). "The high and lofty One that inhabiteth eternity" (Isa. 57:15).

3. *Spirituality.* "God is a Spirit" (John 4:24).

4. *Unity.* There is one true and living God. "There is no God else beside me" (Isa. 45:21).

5. *Immutability.* "I am the Lord, I change not" (Mal. 3:6). "The Father of lights, with whom is no variableness, neither shadow of turning" (Jas. 1:17).

6. *Omnipresence.* He is everywhere present. "Can any hide himself in secret places that I shall not see him? saith the Lord.

Do not I fill heaven and earth?" (Jer. 23:24). He is "not far from every one of us: for in him we live, and move, and have our being" (Acts 17:27-28).

7. *Omniscience.* He is all-knowing. "Known unto God are all his works from the beginning of the world" (Acts 15:18). "Neither is there any creature that is not manifest in his sight: but all things are naked and opened unto the eyes of him with whom we have to do" (Heb. 4:13).

8. *Omnipotence.* He has unlimited and universal power. "His eternal power and Godhead" (Rom. 1:20). "With God all things are possible" (Matt. 19:26).

9. *Wisdom.* "Blessed be the name of God forever and ever: for wisdom and might are his" (Dan. 2:20). "O the depths of the riches both of the wisdom and knowledge of God! How unsearchable are his judgments, and his ways past finding out!" (Rom. 11:33).

10. *Holiness and truth.* "I am holy" (I Pet. 1:16). "Thou art of purer eyes than to behold evil, and canst not look on iniquity" (Hab. 1:13). "God, that cannot lie" (Titus 1:2).

11. *Justice.* God demands righteousness of all his intelligent creatures, and he deals righteously with them. "Justice and judgment are the habitation of thy throne" (Ps. 89:14). "In every nation he that feareth him, and worketh righteousness, is accepted with him" (Acts 10:35).

12. *Goodness.* He is benevolent, loving, merciful, and gracious. "The goodness of God" (Rom. 2:4). "God so loved the world" (John 3:16). "His mercy endureth forever" (Ps. 136:26). "The God of all grace" (I Pet. 5:10).

13. *Faithfulness.* "The Lord is faithful" (II Thess. 3:3). "Sara . . . judged him faithful who had promised" (Heb. 11:11).

The Trinity

The theological term "Trinity" signifies the union of three Persons—Father, Son, and Holy Spirit—in the Godhead. This subject was a most fruitful source of theological controversy in past ages, and even at the present day there are professed Christians who deny the triune nature of God. Our present limits preclude an extended discussion of the matter, but I will bring forward a few points favorable to the doctrine of the Trinity.

Since the exact manner of existence in the Godhead manifestly lies above and beyond the range of mortal mind, the basis of our theology respecting God should be laid solely in what is revealed to us in the Holy Scriptures. And if we appeal directly to them, we find it is impossible to avoid the doctrine of the Trinity without doing great violence to scores of plain texts bearing on the subject. The course of argument is as follows:

1. The Father, the Son, and the Holy Spirit are represented as special Persons distinct from each other.

2. They are classed together, separate from all other beings.

3. Divine titles are applied to each.

4. Divine attributes are ascribed to each.

5. Divine works are attributed to each.

Yet there is only one God.

The Father. The word "Father," referring to the Godhead, is used in Scripture in a twofold sense. First, it is applied to God without any personal distinctions. "Thou art my father, my God, and the rock of my salvation" (Ps. 89:26). (See also John 4:21, 23; and other texts.) Second, it is applied to God in contrast with Christ, who is thus distinguished as Son in his office of Redeemer. "All things are delivered unto me of my Father: and no man knoweth the Son, but the Father" (Matt. 11:27). "Jesus answered them, My Father worketh hitherto, and I work" (John 5:17). (See also Acts 2:32-33; Rom. 15:6; Gal. 1:1-4; and numerous other texts.)

The Son. The passages already cited show that Christ is a person distinct from the Father. The following facts prove scripturally that the Son is divine—equal with the Father himself:

1. *Divine titles are applied to Him the same as to the Father.* "Unto the Son he saith, Thy throne, O God, is forever and ever: a scepter of righteousness is the scepter of thy kingdom" (Heb. 1:18). "The mighty God, The everlasting Father, The Prince of Peace" (Isa. 9:6). "Emmanuel" (Matt. 1:23). (See also Acts 20:28; John 20:28; Rom. 9:5; Phil. 2:6; Col. 2:9; Titus 1:3; I John 5:20; Rev. 17:14; and other texts.)

2. *Divine attributes are ascribed to Him.* The following attributes of God the Father are also ascribed to Jesus Christ

a) *Pre-existence, or eternity.* "Before Abraham was, I am" (John 8:58). "The second man is the Lord from heaven" (I Cor. 15:47). "That which was from the beginning" (I John 1:1). (See also Phil. 2:6-7; John 17:5; Mic. 5:2.) Likewise, in the Revelation Christ is represented by that symbolic title signifying eternity, "Alpha and Omega" (Rev. 22:13). Therefore the statement that Christ is the Son of God doubtless refers specifically to his miraculous virgin birth, thus denoting God's special relation to him in his office work as the world's Redeemer.

b) *Omnipotence.* "The government shall be upon his shoulder" (Isa. 9:6). "Jesus came and spake unto them, saying, All power is given unto me in heaven and in earth" (Matt. 28:18). (See also John 10:17-18; 11:25; Phil. 3:21; Heb. 1:3; II Tim. 1:10.)

c) *Omnipresence.* "Where two or three are gathered together in my name, there am I in the midst of them" (Matt. 18:20). "Lo, I am with you alway, even unto the end of the world" (28:20).

d) *Omniscience.* "He knew all men, and needed not that any should testify of man; for he knew what was in man" (John 2:24-25). "Lord, thou knowest all things" (21:17). "In whom are hid all the treasures of wisdom and knowledge" (Col. 2:3).

Also, holiness, truth, justice, goodness and faithfulness are attributes of Christ. See also chapter 5, under subtitle "Evidences of Christ's Deity."

3. *Divine works are ascribed to Him.* The following works are ascribed to the Son:

a) *Creation.* "God . . . hath in these last days spoken unto us by his Son . . . by whom also he made the worlds" (Heb. 1:1-2). "Thou, Lord, in the beginning hast laid the foundation of the earth; and the heavens are the works of thine hands" (vs. 10). (Also John 1:3; Col. 1:16.)

b) *Redemption.* "In whom we have redemption through his blood, the forgiveness of sins" (Eph. 1:7). This phase will be more fully considered later.

4. *He is pre-eminent—above all things.* "He is Lord of all" (Acts 10: 36). "Lord both of the dead and living" (Rom. 14: 9). (See also Phil. 2: 9; Col. 1: 18; I Pet. 3: 22.)

5. *He is a proper object of devotion and worship.* Though the Scriptures denounce idolatry and enjoin the worship of the one true and living God only, they set forth Christ as a proper object of devotion and worship. "Let all the angels of God worship him" (Heb. 1: 6). "All men should honor the Son, even as they honor the Father" (John 5: 23). "And they worshiped him" (Luke 24: 52). Saints "in every place call upon the name of Jesus Christ our Lord" (I Cor. 1: 2). "At the name of Jesus every knee should bow" (Phil. 2: 10).

The Holy Spirit. The Holy Spirit is also divine and is a distinct person from the Father and the Son. He is called the "Spirit of God" (Rom. 8: 9) because "he proceedeth from the Father" (John 15: 26); also the "Spirit of Christ" (Rom. 8: 9), because he is sent to do the work of Christ.

1. *His deity.* His deity is shown by many texts. "It is not ye that speak, but the Spirit of your Father which speaketh in you" (Matt. 10: 20). Compare Ezekiel 36: 27 with Acts 2: 17-18. (See also Acts 28: 25; Rom. 8: 14; I Cor. 3: 16.)

2. *His personality.* The personality of the Holy Spirit is shown by the following facts:

a) *He is associated with two other persons—Father and Son—as their equal.* "In the name of the Father, and of the Son, and of the Holy Ghost" (Matt. 28: 19).

b) *The personal pronoun "he" is applied to him,* "Howbeit when he, the Spirit of truth, is come, he will guide you into all truth: for he shall not speak of himself; but whatsoever he shall hear, that shall he speak: and he will show you things to come" (John 16: 13).

c) *Personal acts are ascribed to him.* "He shall teach you all things" (John 14: 26). "He shall testify of me" (15: 26). (See also Acts 13: 2, 4.)

d) *Particular attributes are ascribed to him.* For example, knowledge (I Cor. 2: 11), will (12: 11), power (Rom. 15: 13).

3. *His works.* The works of the Holy Spirit are described as follows:

a) *In creation.* "In the beginning God created. . . . And the Spirit of God moved upon the face of the waters" (Gen. 1:1-2). (See also Job 33:4; 26:13; Ps. 104:30.)

b) *In redemption.* "Salvation through sanctification of the Spirit" (II Thess. 2:13). God gave "them the Holy Ghost . . . purifying their hearts by faith" (Acts 15:8-9). "He saved us by the washing of regeneration, and renewing of the Holy Ghost" (Titus 3:5). (See also I John 3:24; Rom. 8:9, 14, 16.)

The Father, the Son, and the Holy Spirit are classed together, separately from all other beings, as divine. "In the name of the Father, and of the Son, and of the Holy Ghost" (Matt. 28:19). "The grace of the Lord Jesus Christ, and the love of God, and the communion of the Holy Ghost, be with you all" (II Cor. 13:14). (See also Jude 20-21; I Pet. 1:2; Rom. 8:14-17; and others.)

God's Works

The following creative acts are ascribed to God:

1. *The creation of angels.* "Bless the Lord, ye his angels, that excel in strength . . . hearkening unto the voice of his word" (Ps. 103:20). (See also Job 38:4, 7; II Thess. 1:7.)

2. *The creation of the material universe.* "In the beginning God created the heaven and the earth" (Gen. 1:1).

3. *The creation of man.* "So God created man in his own image" (Gen. 1:27).

Having created all things, God now controls and conserves all things in his vast universe in accordance with his own will. His intelligent creatures are made the subjects of a moral, providential government.

CONCERNING MAN

Chapter 2

THE NATURE OF MAN

The Origin of Man

Turning to the Bible, we find the only satisfactory account of man's beginning. "So God created man in his own image . . . male and female created he them" (Gen. 1:27). "Have we not all one father? hath not one God created us?" (Mal. 2:10). From the original pair, Adam and Eve, the entire human race has sprung; for Eve is declared to be "the mother of all living" (Gen. 3:20). The Bible writers uniformly acknowledge this common origin of man. Paul affirms that God "hath made of one blood all nations of men . . . for we are also his offspring" (Acts 17:26, 28).

From whatever standpoint we view man, he appears as the special workmanship of God, the highest type of earthly creatures, made "in the image of God," to use the language of the writer of Genesis. This expression, "image of God," is comprehensive. It implies that special characteristics of the Divine One are made a part of man's being. Thus, man *is a moral being*. In his normal state his actions are not determined by mere instinct or expediency or self-interest, but they are regarded as possessing in their own nature a clearly defined rightness or wrongness. In this moral discrimination man is like God. In connection with this, he possesses *freedom of will*, so that he can of his own volition decide his course of conduct. He is also *an intelligent being*, possessing a mind capable of almost infinite development, one which easily grasps the mightiest problems within the range of finite environment. Man is also *a spiritual being*, who naturally looks up to God, "the Father of spirits," as his author and who is capable of holding sweet converse with his Maker.

As a moral and spiritual being in God's likeness, man origi-

17

nally was, of necessity, in a state of holiness and purity. According to the Word, he was placed under moral law. To this day men everywhere realize and admit that they are the subjects of moral government, directly responsible to God. This is also the uniform teaching of the Scriptures. But the same Scriptures also teach that the original state of holiness was forfeited by sin; hence in this respect *and to this extent* the image of God was lost. In the redemption of Christ, however, holiness is regained; therefore, we are restored to the image of God. "Lie not one to another, seeing that ye have put off the old man with his deeds; and have put on the new man, which is renewed in knowledge after the image of him that created him" (Col. 3:9-10). (See also Eph. 4:22-24.)

Man a Compound Being

The Scriptures represent man as a twofold, or dual, being, possessed of body and soul, or body and spirit. "Glorify God in your body, and in your spirit" (I Cor. 6:20). "That she may be holy both in body and in spirit" (7:34). (See also Job 14:22; II Cor. 4:16.)

The "outer man," or body, is mortal: "your mortal body" (Rom. 6:12); "your mortal bodies" (8:11). The body was created in this mortal condition, as the following facts show: (1) It was made out of the dust of the earth (Gen. 2:7); (2) it was to subsist upon natural food (1:29); (3) man was given natural work to perform (2:15); (4) matrimony was instituted (1:27-28). According to the words of Christ, marriage is an institution that does not pertain to angels or to beings wholly immortal, such as we shall be after the resurrection. (See Luke 20:35-36.) (5) There was use for the tree of life (Gen. 3:22). Had man been created with an immortal body, the tree of life would have been entirely useless.

The crowning proof that man was originally mortal is the fact that God "made him a little lower than the angels" (Ps. 8:5; Heb. 2:6-7). In what sense was man lower than the angels? Not morally or spiritually, for in these respects man was in God's image, and surely the angels are not higher than God. What, then, does the expression mean? The writer of Hebrews says that God "maketh his angels spirits" (1:7); that they are "all ministering spirits" (vs. 14). Jesus plainly states that "a spirit hath not flesh and bones" (Luke 24:39). Therefore, we conclude that man's inferiority to angels consists in the limitations necessitated by a physical body, while the angels are wholly spirit beings. That this inference is correct is shown by other Scripture texts. Paul asserts that in the resurrection day "this mortal body must put on immortality" (I Cor. 15:53). Jesus says concerning his people in this "resurrection from the dead," "Neither can they die any more: for they are equal unto the angels" (Luke 20:36).

The question now arises, Why, then, do the Bible writers state that death came upon mankind as a result of sin? The answer: While man remained in the Garden of Eden with free access to the tree of life, his continued existence without death was assured. And when, after the Fall, the decree of death had been pronounced, this decree could be made effective only by depriving him of those privileges which had before sustained life; therefore he was driven from the garden, "lest he put forth his hand, and take also of the tree of life, and eat, and live forever" (Gen. 3:22). The real sentence of God against man as the result of the Fall is expressed in Genesis 3:19, "Dust thou art, and unto dust shalt thou return." In other words, the curse placed upon man was not mortality, but condemnation to the effects of mortality; hence "by man came death."

Since the body of man is by nature mortal, it can be destroyed (Job 19:26); killed (Matt. 10:28); it perishes (II Cor. 4:16); it returns to the dust of the earth (Gen. 3:19).

But is this all there is of man? No! What do the Scriptures say? "Though our outward man perish, yet the inward man is renewed day by day" (II Cor. 4:16). "There is a spirit in man" (Job 32:8). This soul, or spirit, is the creative work of God—"The souls which I have made" (Isa. 57:16). It is the Lord that "layeth the foundation of the earth, and formeth the spirit of man within him" (Zech. 12:1). Our bodies partake of the nature of our earthly fathers, hence are subject to death and decay; while our spirits, made "in the image of God," partake of his essential nature, and "God is a Spirit"—"immortal, invisible" (I Tim. 1:17). Therefore Jesus says plainly,

"Fear not them which kill the body, but are not able to kill the soul" (Matt. 10:28). David affirms, "Your heart shall live forever" (Ps. 22:26).

In language still plainer the Apostle Paul shows that the soul is in its own nature eternal. "Though our outward man perish, yet the inward man is renewed day by day. . . . While we look not at the things which are seen, but at the things which are not seen: for the things which are seen are temporal; but the things which are not seen are eternal" (II Cor. 4:16, 18). (See also 5:1, 6, 8.)

This soul, or spirit, is the knowing, volitional, and responsible part of man. "For what man knoweth the things of a man, save the spirit of man which is in him? even so the things of God knoweth no man, but the Spirit of God" (I Cor. 2:11). Just as the Spirit of God knows the things of God, so the spirit of man knows the things of man. "Shall I give my first born for my transgression, the fruit of my body for the sin of my soul?" (Mic. 6:7). This text fixes responsibility upon the soul; and since the soul is the knowing, volitional part of man, it is the real man. In James 2:26 we read that "the body without the spirit is dead." The Scriptures represent the body as being only the instrument of the soul (Rom. 6:12-13). Every appeal that God makes to man is addressed to the real man—the soul.

This twofoldness of man was represented by Paul (II Cor. 5:1-9) under the figure of a house and its occupant, thus showing their interdependence or relationship in the present state, wherein the spirit is in union with the natural body. But he goes further and shows that the house is not indispensable to the existence of the occupant; that when it is "dissolved" the real man is "absent from the body" and "present with the Lord." Peter also describes the present union with the natural body and the separation at death under the same figure (II Pet. 1:13-14). It is sometimes affirmed that a man is nothing without his body, but it is evident from II Corinthians 12:2-4 that Paul had no such belief; for here he describes one who was caught up to paradise, and there saw and heard and understood certain things, yet he did not know whether the person was in the body or out of the body at that time. Paul believed that man is a dual being—that man can be separated from his body and still be a seeing, knowing, thinking creature. It is evident from Philippians 1:21-24 that to die meant, to the Apostle, to leave the flesh, to "depart, and to be with Christ."

In Jesus' account of Lazarus and the rich man (Luke 16:19-31), we have this same doctrine of the survival of the spirit after death. It is useless to attempt to evade the force of this passage by asserting, as do some, that it is "only a parable." It is not so stated. "There was a certain rich man . . . and there was a certain beggar named Lazarus."

When Christ took Peter, James, and John up into a mountain and was transfigured before them, we are told that "there appeared unto them Moses and Elias talking with him" (Matt. 17:1-3). The Bible records that Elias (Elijah) was translated; it also states that Moses "died in the land of Moab" and was buried "in a valley" (Deut. 34:5-6). Now, how did it happen that Moses appeared here on the mount? He had not been resurrected from the dead into this glorified state, for the Scriptures declare that Christ was the first one to receive this change. Some people who had recently died were restored to life before Christ's resurrection, but that was only a restoration of the natural, corruptible body *on the earth,* and these persons were subject to death again. The true "resurrection from the dead," which places men in an incorruptible state, is different from this. Therefore Christ was the "first begotten of the dead" (Rev. 1:5); "the first born from the dead" (Col. 1:18); "the first fruits of them that slept" (I Cor. 15:20). The transfiguration was before the death and resurrection of Christ, therefore the decomposed body of Moses had not been brought forth from the dead. The fact that Moses appeared on the Mount of Transfiguration hundreds of years after his death shows clearly that his soul was not involved in the ruin of his body.

Jesus taught that the ancient patriarchs were still living. (See Matt. 22:31-32.) John in apocalyptic vision saw disembodied souls (Rev. 6:9-10; 20:4).

Natural death is the separation of body and spirit. To the dying thief, Christ said, "Today shalt thou be with me in paradise"; and in his last moment he cried out, "Father, into thy hands I commend my spirit" (Luke 23:43, 46). The dying Stephen said, "Lord Jesus, receive my spirit" (Acts 7:59). This doctrine of the survival of the spirit is found throughout the Bible. (See Gen. 35:18; Pss. 23:4; 90:10; Eccles. 12:7; Matt. 10:28; Phil. 1:21, 23; II Cor. 5:8.)

The dying testimonies of thousands of saints confirm the doctrine of the Scriptures on this point—that at death the soul takes its departure from the body to be in a more sacred nearness with the Lord. In the most solemn hour of life this truth is so firmly stamped upon the heart that it finds expression in language unmistakable.

Objections Considered

Now, what can be brought against this solid array of Scripture texts teaching the dual nature of man? Nothing except a few obscure texts which usually refer to some other subject. The strongest text that can be used for that purpose is Ecclesiastes 9:5: "The dead know not anything." True, that part of man which dies and goes into the grave knows nothing; but what about that part of his being that flies away at death, returns to "God who gave it," rests "with Christ, which is far better," and is "eternal" (II Cor. 4:18)? This statement that the dead know not anything, however, is qualified in the following verse by the words, "Neither have they any more a portion forever in anything that is done under the sun" (Eccles. 9:6). This agrees perfectly with certain other uses of this expression in the Bible. For example, II Samuel 15:11: "And with Absalom went two hundred men out of Jerusalem, that were called; and they went in their simplicity, and they knew not anything." This text does not signify that they knew absolutely nothing, but simply indicates that they were altogether ignorant concerning the particular thing under consideration—Absalom's conspiracy. (See also I Sam. 20:39; I Tim. 6:4.)

It is sometimes urged that Christ "only hath immortality" (I Tim. 6:16). The terms "mortal" and "immortal" are in the Scriptures applied to bodily conditions rather than to the soul, hence have no bearing whatever on the question of the soul's inherent nature. It is the body that is mortal (the soul is *never* described by this term), and "this mortal must put on immortality." Christ rose from the dead with a glorified, immortalized body, "the first fruits of them that sleep," "death hath no more dominion over him"; therefore he "only hath immortality."

The so-called death of the soul, often spoken of in the Bible, is not the end of its conscious existence, but is simply spiritual death—spiritual separation from God *in this present world*. "The soul that sinneth, it shall die" (Ezek. 18:20). "Dead in trespasses and sins; wherein in time past ye walked" (Eph. 2:1-2). The soul was dead—dead in a spiritual sense—and yet the individual was alive and walking around on the earth. "Dead while she liveth" (I Tim. 5:6). Many texts could be given on this point.

I have dwelt at some length on this point concerning the nature of man because of its importance in the plan of redemption. Those who deny the doctrine of the actual essential nature of soul, or spirit, as being by nature deathless, are led by logical necessity to deny also the doctrine of the new birth and the reception of eternal life *in this world*; for how can it be said that man now possesses eternal life if death ends all until the day of resurrection?

CONCERNING THE PROBLEM OF SIN

Chapter 3

THE PROBLEM OF SIN

The presence of moral evil in God's universe is one of the great questions that has puzzled the mind of man. The Bible represents God as a being almighty in power, intrinsically good, and holy in all his works; nevertheless, we are confronted by the stupendous fact of sin in the world. Whence came it?

The Origin of Sin

The subject of the origin of moral evil and the reason for its existence naturally resolves itself into one of the three following positions, each of which has been earnestly maintained by many people: (1) that God is the direct author of sin and is alone responsible for it, man being but an irresponsible agent in carrying out His will; (2) that God has seen fit to employ sin as his method to bring about certain good results not otherwise obtainable—a view somewhat related to the first position; (3) that moral evil is in no sense according to God's will and forms no part of his plans, his purposes, or his ways; that it originated in the finite and by apostasy from God, and that, therefore, God is not responsible for it, but all his relations to it are antagonistic and in the way of prevention, remedy, or punishment.

The first position—that God is the direct author of sin— is opposed to every revelation which God has made of himself in his Word. It is also irreconcilable with reason and the inner moral sense of mankind.

God is the author of what is termed "physical evil"; therefore we read, "I make peace, and create evil: I the Lord do all these things" (Isa. 45:7); "Shall there be evil in a city, and the Lord hath not done it?" (Amos 3:6). Such evil consists of temporal punishments or judgments that God brings upon men because of their sins (Jonah 3:10). God is not the author of moral evil, or sin; he is infinitely holy. One should not charge upon God, "that cannot lie" (Titus 1:2), all the falsehoods that have been uttered during the ages; nor state that the Holy One, who is "of purer eyes than to behold evil, and canst not look on iniquity" (Hab. 1:13), is, after all, its direct cause.

The second position—that sin is God's choice of methods for bringing about the greatest good—has had a larger number of supporters. They assume that although sin is contrary to the nature of God it is nevertheless according to his will that men should sin in order that his glorious power may be manifested in bringing into effect the plan of redemption, so that the sinner can experience the exquisite delights and enjoyments of contrast by being saved from sin. But if all this be necessary in order to insure happiness to finite beings, the angels of heaven must be very miserable; for as far as we know they have never had the privilege of experiencing this blessedness of contrast!

The Bible nowhere introduces sin as God's work or method. Can God consistently decree that we shall sin, and at the same time prohibit us from doing it and threaten us with the direst punishments if we do?

The third position harmonizes with the moral sense in man, with the plain teachings of the Word, and with all the known facts in the case. Moral evil is contrary to God's nature, contrary to his plans, his purposes, and his ways. All his relations to it are antagonistic. It *originated in the finite and by apostasy from God.*

God being holy, he could no more make a sinful being than he could lie (which is declared to be impossible); for God is a power only in the direction of his own nature and attributes. But an intelligent being much like himself he could and did make. Intelligence, however, implies real *cause,* that the being so endowed possesses inherently the power of acting voluntarily. Without this element of freedom, this power of choice and determination of conduct, true intelligence and moral responsibility could not exist.

With man possessing within himself the principle of *cause* as truly as does his Maker, so that he must act voluntarily, we see at once that it is within his sphere also to act wrongly. In other words, the *possibility* of sin inheres in all finite moral beings; for manifestly it is impossible to do right voluntarily without possessing the ability also to do wrong. This is the gist of the whole argument. The problem of sin is a problem of moral government. The individual with a personal will possesses a method and purpose exclusively his own. God is in no wise responsible for it. God having created man intelligent, in His own image, His responsibility in this respect ceased. The universe as a physical unit was incomplete, but when peopled with moral beings capable of rendering intelligent, voluntary service to God, the plan was perfect; therefore, man stands out as the crowning work of God's creative effort.

Sin and Predestination

The first chapters of Genesis give an account of how sin was introduced into this part of God's moral universe. It occurred by the willful choice of our foreparents, and by this means they apostatized from God. Ever since that time God's relations to evil have been antagonistic, in the way of prevention, remedy, and punishment. Even those individuals who have unconsciously fulfilled some part of God's plan in his relations to sin have at the same time acted *voluntarily*.

These thoughts, carefully considered, explain what is one of the most difficult texts in the Bible pertaining to this subject—Acts 2:23: "Him, being delivered by the determinate counsel and foreknowledge of God, ye have taken, and by wicked hands have crucified and slain." Here the Apostle Peter charges the Jews with the most atrocious wickedness in crucifying the Son of God, and yet in the same verse teaches that it was according to God's will that Christ should die. The purpose these men had in the act was evil, and they alone were responsible for it; therefore God, knowing their designs, simply delivered Christ into their hands, thus accomplishing his own purpose without violating in the least their free moral agency.

God claims no responsibility for men's methods and action, except in his proper relations to them. (See Isa. 55:8.) Yet some would have us believe that everything that men do is in some secret and unexplainable manner according to the will of God. It is not true. Men's methods may or may not be in accordance with the will of God. Through the exercise of an overruling Providence all things are made to "work together for good to them that love God" (Rom. 8:28), but even here the principle of free moral agency is respected, so that men's moral actions result from their own voluntary desires.

The Nature of Sin

Two verses of Scripture give us a correct interpretation of sin. "Whosoever committeth sin transgresseth also the law: for sin is the transgression of the law" (I John 3:4). "Therefore to him that knoweth to do good, and doeth it not, to him it is sin" (Jas. 4:17). Sin is therefore either the conscious, voluntary transgression of God's law or else the willful failure to conform to its requirements. God's law is an infinite law; therefore its violation becomes a serious offense, involving the soul in spiritual ruin, both in time and in eternity. "Is not thy wickedness great? and thine iniquities infinite?" (Job 22:5). The first transgression by our foreparents caused their banishment from Eden and the consequent train of sickness, pain, sorrow, and death.

The Universality of Sin

The consciousness of sin is universal, all men having fallen under its dismal and blighting sway. One of the main arguments of Paul in the Roman letter was to show that all men are sinners, in order that he might emphasize the truth of Christ's mission as the universal Savior. Listen to his conclusion: "We have before proved both Jews and Gentiles, that they are all under sin" (Rom. 3:9); "There is no difference: for all have sinned, and come short of the glory of God" (vss. 22-23).

CONCERNING REDEMPTION

Chapter 4

THE REDEMPTIVE PLAN

The fall of man wrought a radical change in his nature and condition; the primitive purity was lost, and sin and condemnation rested upon his guilty soul. As a result, the entire race was plunged into sin; therefore all men stand in need of redemption.

Self-Redemption Impossible

Redemption would imply a return to the original perfect state, in both character and condition, and this restoration man could not of his own will effect. In the first place, there was a legal difficulty that he could not surmount. As a moral being, he had been placed under moral law, and this law required his perfect obedience. Its requirements might all be summed up in the words, "Thou shalt love the Lord thy God with all thy heart, and with all thy soul, and with all thy mind" (Matt. 22:37). Having disobeyed, man could not make reparation for his transgressions, since no surplus obedience is possible.

Also, there was an insurmountable moral difficulty. Having lost purity and innocence, man could not by self-effort regain them. "Who can bring a clean thing out of an unclean? not one" (Job 14:4). Yet such a restoration is indispensable to redemption. "Except a man be born again, he cannot see the kingdom of God" (John 3:3). "Follow peace with all men, and holiness, without which no man shall see the Lord" (Heb. 12:14). Self-redemption was therefore clearly impossible.

Will God Redeem?

As set forth in the previous chapter God stands acquitted of all responsibility in the Fall. Is there any evidence that he will redeem? The universal prevalence of sacrifices testifies that men have in all ages believed that God would redeem. It is highly probable that this practice was instituted by God's appointment (Gen. 3:21 with 4:4). If so, then we have in this a clear evidence of God's redemptive purpose.

A Divine Plan Progressively Revealed

Revelation itself, however, makes this subject clear. There existed in the divine mind a plan of restoration for fallen man. "Then began men to call upon the name of the Lord" (Gen. 4:26). A little later "Enoch walked with God" (5:24); while to Noah, God manifested himself particularly. These facts show God's attitude toward the race.

When we come forward to the time of Abraham, we find a remarkable revelation of the plan of redemption in the special covenant that God made with the father of the Hebrew nation. This covenant consisted of two parts. The first part related to Abraham and his literal seed: God would make of him a great nation; his descendants should sojourn for a time in a strange land, after which God would bring them into the land of Canaan and give it to them for their inheritance. The second part of the covenant was of a spiritual nature, for in Abraham and his seed all the families of the earth were to be blessed (Gen. 12:1-3; 13:14-15; 15:5, 13-16; 17:1-8; 22:17-18).

This second division of the covenant so clearly depicted Christ and his universal gospel that Jesus said, "Abraham rejoiced to see my day: and he saw it, and was glad" (John 8:56). Paul says: "Now to Abraham and his seed were the promises made. He saith not, And to seeds, as of many; but as of one, And to thy seed, which is Christ." "That the blessing of Abraham might come on the Gentiles through Jesus Christ; that we might receive the promise of the Spirit through faith" (Gal. 3:16, 14). (See also Rom. 4:13, 16-17.)

In the fulfillment of the first part of this covenant to Abraham's seed, God gave the Law of Moses, the ostensible object of which was to govern and benefit the Israelitish nation, but the greatest object of which was doubtless to furnish a system of types and shadows—of sacrifices and ceremonies, offerings and oblations—pointing forward to the second division of the covenant, when the spiritual and real worship of God would be established among the nations of the earth. This law, and the manner in which it was delivered, imparted a clearer revelation of God's nature and character, as well as of his plan, and thus furnished the means of disciplining the Jews in preparation for the coming Messiah.

The later prophets were not limited to an external system of types and shadows, but the Spirit of God made known to them directly the higher standard of revelation to be brought about by Christ. Isaiah says that "God . . . will come and save you" (35:4) and that this salvation will be effected by His vicarious suffering and death (Chap. 53). Daniel predicted that the Messiah would come "to finish the transgression, and to make an end of sins, and to make reconciliation for iniquity, and to bring in everlasting righteousness" (9:24). Joel prophesied that in the last days God would pour out his Spirit upon all flesh (2:28-29). Zechariah pointed to the fountain of cleansing for sin and uncleanness that would be "opened to the house of David" (13:1).

Jesus Christ brought the highest revelation of God and taught a proper standard of human conduct, but above all we find in him God's perfect remedy for sin. He came "to save his people from their sins" (Matt. 1:21; I John 3:5-6). Thus, the moral restoration of man to the original condition of holiness and purity is accomplished (Titus 2:14).

The redemptive plan was not completely fulfilled, however, at the time of Christ's first advent. So far as the soul is concerned, the means was provided for its moral restoration; but we have seen that the Fall affected man physically also. It was doubtless God's original design "that mortality might be swallowed up of life"—that mortal man in the Garden of Eden should, by partaking of the tree of life, maintain his natural life indefinitely, until such time as it pleased God to translate or immortalize him. Since this purpose was frustrated through sin, it has now become a part of the redemptive plan "that mortality might be swallowed up of life" (II Cor. 5:4). And since, because of original sin, it has been "appointed unto men once to die" (Heb. 9:27), that part of the redemptory scheme relative to our immortalization has been deferred until the last great day, the day of resurrection, when "this corruptible

must put on incorruption, and this mortal must put on immortality" (I Cor. 15:53).

Paul recognizes the fact that our bodies are included in the
redemptive work, for he says, "Know ye not that your body
is the temple of the Holy Ghost? . . . For ye are bought with
a price: therefore glorify God in your body, and in your spirit,
which are God's (I Cor. 6:19-20). (See also Eph. 1:13-14; II Cor.
5:1-5; Rom. 8:23.)

A knowledge of this progressive feature of God's redemptive
work is necessary to a correct understanding of what the Bible
really teaches. God's method of revelation was adjusted to the
nature and the condition of men, and was therefore progressive, so that at times one part was made to succeed another
part, but progress was always upward. The unity that we find
in all parts of the Bible is a *unity of purpose and plan, which
God was constantly seeking to make known to man* and by
which man was being gradually elevated, that is, the redemptive plan.

Chapter 5

CHRIST AND THE ATONEMENT

The Incarnation

The word "incarnation," derived from Latin, signifies "in the flesh." To become incarnate, then, signifies to become a man. So long as Christ remained in the sphere of absolute Godhead, he could not be subject to the jurisdiction of his own objective law; neither could he in any sense directly affect man in the way of redemption, there being no point of contact with man. He could not cease to be God and thus become a mere creature under the law's jurisdiction, but it was possible for him to come out of the sphere of absolute Godhead into the sphere of real manhood by assuming human form and human nature in connection with his deity. "Forasmuch then as the children are partakers of flesh and blood, he also himself likewise took part of the same. . . . For verily he took not on him the nature of angels; but he took on him the seed of Abraham" (Heb. 2:14, 16).

To reject the doctrine of the incarnation is, in effect, to reject the whole Bible; for not only does the New Testament revolve around the Person of Christ as God incarnate, but the Old Testament stands committed to the same truth, because it contains direct prophecies of the incarnation. (See Isa. 9:6-7; 7:14; Mic. 5:2.) If these texts do not teach the earthly birth of a divine being, it would be difficult to state such a fact. Some professing Christians have been rather inclined to doubt the story of the virgin birth, but it seems to me that if the divine was to become human, nothing could be more natural than that his introduction to this world of sin should occur in some extraordinary manner.

The special evidences of Christ's deity are so numerous that I can refer to only a few of them.

1. *The prophecies of the incarnation.* These were all fulfilled in Christ. He was born of a virgin (Isa. 7:14) in Bethlehem (Mic. 5:2). The Old Testament abounds in prophecies concern-

ing the birth, ministry, mission, death, and resurrection of the Messiah—more than three hundred in all—and all were completely fulfilled in Jesus of Nazareth. To these prophecies more than to all else the first preachers appealed in establishing the Messiahship of Jesus (e.g., Acts 18:28).

2. *The types of the Old Testament.* These were fulfilled in Christ. The blood of the sacrificial victims, which from the days of Abel had flowed freely in atonement for the sins of men, pointed forward unmistakably to a great Sacrifice, even the sacrifice of our Lord.

3. *The divine names.* Christ bore the divine names "Jehovah," "God," "Emmanuel," "Lord of all," "the mighty God," "everlasting Father," "the true God," "King of kings, and Lord of lords."

4. *Divine attributes.* For a discussion of the divine attributes ascribed to Christ see chapter 1, under sidehead "The Son."

5. *Divine works and miracles.* Christ claimed "power on earth to forgive sins," thus showing that he is God. He turned water into wine, multiplied loaves and fishes, walked on the raging waves of Galilee, and stilled its storms, thus proving that he is Lord of creation. He cast out evil spirits, healed the bodies of the sick and suffering, and even raised the dead, thus demonstrating his universal dominion.

6. *Divine honors.* Christ claimed equality with the Father (John 5:19) and a divine glory with the Father "before the world was" (17:5). He taught that "all men should honor the Son, even as they honor the Father" (5:23). These claims to divine honors were all recognized by the Apostles, who united in the worship of Jesus as the only one through whom salvation could be obtained (Acts 4:12). Paul declared that "at the name of Jesus every knee should bow, of things in heaven, and things in earth, and things under the earth; and that every tongue should confess that Jesus Christ is Lord, to the glory of God the Father" (Phil. 2:10-11).

7. *Unexampled human character.* Christ's life was one of freedom from sin. Not one blot or sin rests upon his character. In the face of his enemies he could say, "Which of you convinceth me of sin?" (John 8:46). If men do not believe in his virgin birth, let them account for his virgin life; for his

life was one of absolute holiness and perfection. In this he differs from all other men, not only in degree, but also *in kind;* for all others possess the nature of evil and "have sinned, and come short of the glory of God." Jesus was the only sinless one who has ever trod this earth of ours. In this he appears more than human.

8. *His death and resurrection.* The trial and crucifixion of Jesus reveal a character more than human. Though mocked and abused, he betrayed no trace of anger or resentment. Nailed to a cross, and expiring in frightful agonies, he pronounced no words of hatred or revenge upon his malignant foes, but instead prayed, "Father, forgive them, for they know not what they do."

The resurrection of Christ is the grand climax of all. This historical event has never been affected by the soldiers' false reports at the time or by the vain reasonings of unbelievers since. The risen Lord appeared after his resurrection to hundreds of people. When Paul stood before King Agrippa and declared that Christ had suffered and risen from the dead, he said, "I am persuaded that none of these things are hidden from him; for this thing was not done in a corner" (Acts 26: 26). Had the Apostles desired to establish a falsehood concerning the resurrection, they would have selected some place other than Jerusalem to begin their deception; for all the facts were easily obtainable there at that time. And it must be remembered also that the Apostles and other Christians gave their own lives in defense of the doctrine of a risen Christ.

The Atonement

"We also joy in God through our Lord Jesus Christ, by whom we have now received the atonement" (Rom. 5: 11). Christianity is based upon the death of Christ as the one great atonement for the sins of men.

The Bible plainly teaches that more than a mere example of piety was required in order to effect our salvation. "For if, when we were enemies, we were reconciled to God by the death of his Son, much more, being reconciled, we shall be saved by his life" (Rom. 5: 10). If sinful men were to reform and then follow perfectly the outward example of Christ's

right doing, this course would in nowise dispose of the sins
of their past life; for men cannot have surplus obedience as a
result of their present righteousness and thus make reparation
for their sins. But "Christ died for our sins according to the
scriptures" (I Cor. 15:3). Those who repent and are converted
have their sins "blotted out," yea, they are washed from their
sins in his own blood (Rev. 1:5).

According to the foregoing considerations, we see that the
necessity of incarnation and atonement lay in the fact of sin.
As a result of the atonement God can be "just, and the justifier of him which believeth in Jesus" (Rom. 3:26). This shows
that God could not be just (maintain his just and holy law)
and pardon men without a ransom price. Man could not ransom himself—the price was too great; angels could not; but,
thank God, he "so loved the world, that he gave his only begotten Son, that whosoever believeth in him should not perish,
but have everlasting life" (John 3:16).

Christ as God could satisfy the claims of infinite justice;
therefore the way of redemption was made possible. Being an
infinite sacrifice, he could pay the debt to infinite justice for
all men. It is the *character of the sacrifice itself* that makes
the atonement of such infinite worth. In the exact use of the
term, God does not "pardon" sin at all, for infinite justice has
exacted the penalty for all committed sins. The forgiveness of
sins which God grants is "for Christ's sake" (Eph. 4:32), "who
. . . bare our sins in his own body on the tree" (I Pet. 2:24).

While one purpose of the atonement is to change the relation of God with men, it is also designed to change the attitude of men toward God. When the transgressor is made to
realize the awful nature and extent of his sin, and to see that
he is deserving of infinite punishment, his heart sinks in de-
spair. If his attention is then turned to Calvary, to the dying
agonies of the God-man, as the one who "gave himself for us,"
hope revives, love for the Redeemer springs up in the sin-
benighted soul, and faith lays hold on the Savior of men, with
the glorious result that the blood washes away the guilt of all
past transgressions. Hallelujah! Then he is ready to exclaim as
did the Apostle John, "We love him, because he first loved
us" (I John 4:19). This is the secret of regeneration.

Chapter 6

CONDITIONS FOR SALVATION

The mission of Christ was "to save his people from their sins" (Matt. 1:21). We have seen that man is universally lost in sin, but that a way of restoration to holiness has been provided through Jesus Christ, and that it rests upon his atonement. Thus far our attention has been directed mainly to the divine side, but there is also a human side to the realization of redemptive blessings.

It is the uniform testimony of the New Testament that salvation is a matter of individual choice. All its offers and promises are addressed to the individual himself for decision, and all the blame for neglect or rejection is laid upon him. "Come unto me, all ye that labor and are heavy laden, and I will give you rest" are the words of the Savior (Matt. 11:28). "If any man thirst, let him come unto me, and drink" (John 7:37). (See also Rev. 3:20; 22:17; John 5:40; Matt. 23:37-38; Heb. 2:3.)

Salvation is the most important subject in the world. It should concern every one of us, for without it our souls will be lost through a never-ending eternity. And since it is offered to man conditionally, how important it is that we understand these conditions in order that we may approach God in an acceptable manner and receive this greatest of gifts!

A Spiritual Awakening

Sin produces spiritual death to the soul. "Your iniquities have separated between you and your God" (Isa. 59:2), and this separation is represented as death (Eph. 2:1; Col. 2:13; I Tim. 5:6). Men become "hardened through the deceitfulness of sin" (Heb. 3:13). "Even their mind and conscience is defiled" (Titus 1:15). They sink into the darkness of a sinful night until, in many cases, there seems to be "no fear of God before their eyes," or until they appear to lose all consciousness of "the exceeding sinfulness of sin." Such people *must be-*

36

come awakened now from their sleep of sin, or else the thunders of judgment will arouse them when it is too late. "Awake to righteousness, and sin not" (I Cor. 15:34).

The true preaching of the gospel of Christ is designed to awaken souls. "For the word of God is quick, and powerful, and sharper than any two-edged sword, piercing even to the dividing asunder of soul and spirit, and of the joints and marrow, and is a discerner of the thoughts and intents of the heart. Neither is there any creature that is not manifest in his sight: but all things are naked and opened unto the eyes of him with whom we have to do" (Heb. 4:12-13).

Desire and Decision

The individual who is aroused to the condemnation resting upon his guilty soul is in a good condition to cry, as did the Philippian jailer, "What must I do to be saved?" (Acts 16:30). He must desire salvation in order to obtain it, and he must decide to meet the required conditions set forth in the Bible.

Godly Sorrow

The sinner must give up the love of sin, despise sin because God does, and feel keenly a sense of sorrow for all the sins he has committed. "For godly sorrow worketh repentance to salvation not to be repented of: but the sorrow of the world worketh death" (II Cor. 7:10). Here godly sorrow is contrasted with the "sorrow of the world." Godly sorrow does not proceed from human exposure of wrong conduct, but is an internal realization of the soul's guilt in the sight of God, accompanied by a *deep sense of regret* for the wrongs committed. This kind of sorrow works repentance.

Repentance

The term "repentance" includes a sense of personal guilt, of grief over sin, hatred toward it, and a *resolute turning from it;* hence all the conditions of salvation may properly be termed the way of repentance. But the most prominent idea is that of the forsaking of sin. "Repent ye therefore, and be converted, that your sins may be blotted out" (Acts 3:19).

"Let the wicked forsake his way, and the unrighteous man his thoughts: and let him return unto the Lord, and he will have mercy upon him; and to our God, for he will abundantly pardon" (Isa. 55:7). All unnatural, enslaving, and evil habits must be utterly forsaken; then God will deliver the individual from their power.

Listen to the Scripture: "If I regard iniquity in my heart, the Lord will not hear me" (Ps. 66:18). If we excuse sin in our hearts and lives and expect to continue in it, we may pray as long as we live, but God will pay no attention to our prayers. In Malachi 2:13 we read of some people who were "covering the altar of the Lord with tears, with weeping, and with crying out," and still he would not regard them, for their hearts were not right. But the "broken spirit: a broken and a contrite heart"—the truly penitent heart—God will not despise (Ps. 51:17). When men become broken in spirit and filled with remorse and sorrow, when they realize their lost and undone condition without Christ, then there is hope for them in God. Bless his name!

Confession

Confession also is required. "He that covereth his sins shall not prosper: but whoso confesseth and forsaketh them shall have mercy" (Prov. 28:13). Many people tremble under the Holy Ghost preaching of the Word and realize their lost condition in sin, but are unwilling to confess their sins as the Bible requires.

To whom must confession be made? First, to the Lord. "If we confess our sins, he is faithful and just to forgive us our sins" (I John 1:9). Why should confession be made to him? Does he not know all about us before we confess? Yes, he understands us altogether. But here is one reason: God has set his standard of right and wrong, thus defining sin; but sinful men set their own standards and attempt to justify themselves accordingly. Now, if such people seek for salvation from God while setting their own standard as to what constitutes sin, God will never hear them. They must acknowledge the standard God has set.

In the second place, confession must be made to men—when

our sins involve them. As the object of confession of sins to God is that we may be reconciled to him, so also the object of confession to people whom we have wronged is that a perfect reconciliation may be effected. God requires us, as say the Scriptures, "to have always a conscience void of offense toward God, and toward men" (Acts 24:16).

Confession to our fellow men is plainly taught by Jesus in the Sermon on the Mount: "Therefore if thou bring thy gift to the altar, and there rememberest that thy brother hath ought against thee; leave there thy gift before the altar, and go thy way; first be reconciled to thy brother, and then come and offer thy gift" (Matt. 5:23-24).

Restitution

But this is not all. The words of Christ were, "Be reconciled." Now, reconciliation may in some cases require more than a mere confession of wrongdoing. If, for example, one man has defrauded another out of twenty dollars, acknowledgment of the wrong deed may need to be accompanied by the money in order to effect a proper reconciliation. This the Bible teaches. "If the wicked restore the pledge, give again that he had robbed, walk in the statutes of life, without committing iniquity; he shall surely live, he shall not die" (Ezek. 33:15). God requires those who desire life to set right their former wrongs and then to walk before God "without committing iniquity" any more.

In some cases, however, such restitution may be altogether impossible. If a man has wrongly taken so much that he is unable to restore all, it is reasonable to suppose that if he will humbly do all he can God will receive him. A text of Scripture, though pertaining directly to another subject, may perhaps cover in principle such a case as this: "If there be first a willing mind, it is accepted according to that a man hath, and not according to that he hath not" (II Cor. 8:12).

Furthermore, many personal wrongs do not rest on a financial basis and cannot be made right by the mere giving of money. The guilty person can acknowledge his wrong and bitterly repent of it, but this is all he can do, and if he is ever saved, he must come in on mercy alone.

Forgiveness

Sometimes the matter is reversed; instead of the seeker having wrongs to set right, he has been wronged by others and has treasured up in his heart feelings of bitterness and enmity toward the offenders. Unless these feelings are given up, they will forever bar the soul from reconciliation with God; for he absolutely refuses to deal with us until our relations with our fellow men are of the kind set forth in the Scriptures. Hear the words of Christ: "If ye forgive not men their trespasses, neither will your Father forgive your trespasses"; but, "If ye forgive men their trespasses, your heavenly Father will also forgive you" (Matt. 6:15, 14). Jesus set an example of the proper attitude toward enemies. When dying on Calvary's cross, he did not call down upon his persecutors the fiercest maledictions of heaven, but tenderly prayed, "Father, forgive them; for they know not what they do" (Luke 23:34). The salvation of Jesus Christ leaves no place in the human heart for that which is sinful; therefore every bad act must be forsaken, as well as every evil affection—bitterness, hardness, hatred, and enmity.

Prayer and Faith

The way is now open for the seeker to find access to God by asking for the pardon that the soul craves. The Lord has instructed him to ask. "Ask, and it shall be given you; seek, and ye shall find; knock, and it shall be opened unto you" (Matt. 7:7). "The same Lord over all is rich unto all that call upon him. For whosoever shall call upon the name of the Lord shall be saved" (Rom. 10:12-13).

Our prayers for salvation must be accompanied by definite faith. "Repentance toward God, and faith toward our Lord Jesus Christ" (Acts 20:21) is the gospel direction for obtaining this desired blessing. When the penitent Philippian jailer cried out, "What must I do to be saved?" the answer was quickly given—"Believe on the Lord Jesus Christ, and thou shalt be saved" (16:30-31). But if the heart is rebellious and unwilling to measure to the requirements laid down in the Word, saving faith will be impossible. We read of one class of people who would not repent so that they could believe (Matt. 21:32). Obedience to the Word places us on believing grounds, where prayer and faith become perfectly natural. Then "if thou shalt confess with thy mouth the Lord Jesus, and shalt believe in thine heart that God hath raised him from the dead, thou shalt be saved. For with the heart man believeth unto righteousness; and with the mouth confession is made unto salvation" (Rom. 10:9-10).

Chapter 7

SALVATION

A Present Possibility

The New Testament throughout speaks of salvation as obtainable by men in their present state on the earth. When the Philippian jailer asked, "What must I do to be saved?" the answer was quickly given, "Believe on the Lord Jesus Christ, and thou shalt be saved" (Acts 16:30-31). Paul said: "I am not ashamed of the gospel of Christ: for it is the power of God unto salvation to everyone that believeth" (Rom. 1:16). (See also Rom. 10:9; I Cor. 1:21.) And in language still more emphatic he declared, "Behold, now is the accepted time; behold, now is the day of salvation" (II Cor. 6:2).

One of the best proofs that salvation is a present possibility is the fact that some have already obtained it. In II Timothy 1:9 Paul affirms that God "hath saved us, and called us with an holy calling." Peter writes to certain brethren who had received "the end of your faith, even the salvation of your souls" (I Pet. 1:9). Paul refers to the work Christ wrought in human hearts in these words: "According to his mercy he saved us, by the washing of regeneration, and renewing of the Holy Ghost" (Titus 3:5); "By grace ye are saved" (Eph. 2:5, 8); "For the preaching of the cross is to them that perish foolishness; but unto us which are saved it is the power of God" (I Cor. 1:18).

What Salvation Means

But what does this term "salvation" signify? Its literal meaning is *deliverance;* hence, in its spiritual usage it signifies *deliverance from sin.* Let the Word of God define its meaning: "Thou shalt call his name Jesus: for he shall save his people from their sins" (Matt. 1:21); "Ye know that he was manifested to take away our sins" (I John 3:5); "For this purpose the Son of God was manifested, that he might destroy the works of the devil" (vs. 8); He "gave himself for our sins, that he might deliver us from this present evil world" (Gal.

42

1:4); "If we confess our sins, he is faithful and just to forgive us our sins, and to cleanse us from all unrighteousness" (I John 1:9). Yea, he hath "loved us, and washed us from our sins in his own blood" (Rev. 1:5).

If the actual results of salvation are not accomplished in the heart and life, then it is because the person is not yet saved. Many people who are still continuing to do the works of sin claim to be Christians, declaring that they are "saved by faith" or are "sinners saved by grace." Now, how can a person be saved by faith or by grace while at the same time he is not saved at all? Salvation is received by faith, but a definite result is obtained, for we receive the end, or object of our faith, which is the salvation of our souls. (See I Pet. 1:9.) Of what use is a mere profession of religion unless one has a real experience in the soul?

Notice how the Apostle Paul also connects salvation with its results in the individual heart and life: "For the grace of God that bringeth salvation hath appeared to all men, teaching us that, denying ungodliness and worldly lusts, we should live soberly, righteously, and godly, in this present world; looking for that blessed hope, and the glorious appearing of the great God and our Savior Jesus Christ; who gave himself for us, that he might redeem us from all iniquity, and purify unto himself a peculiar people, zealous of good works" (Titus 2:11-14).

In the Scriptures salvation is described by different terms, as justification, conversion, and the new birth, each of which conveys a certain special idea relative to the subject. The reader must understand, however, that all these terms used in the remainder of this chapter relate to but one work—the first work of grace. For example, we are not justified at one time, converted at another time, receive the new birth at another time; these terms express only different aspects of the same work.

We will consider *justification* first. This is the legal aspect. To justify means to absolve from guilt. "All have sinned, and come short of the glory of God; being justified freely by his grace, through the redemption that is in Christ Jesus: whom God hath set forth to be a propitiation through faith in his blood, to declare his righteousness . . . that he might be just, and the justifier of him which believeth in Jesus. . . . Therefore we conclude that a man is justified by faith" (Rom. 3:23-28).

God "made him to be sin for us, who knew no sin; that we might be made the righteousness of God in him" (II Cor. 5:21). "Therefore being justified by faith, we have peace with God through our Lord Jesus Christ" (Rom. 5:1).

Widely prevalent in Christendom is a false and deceptive doctrine to the effect that Christians can continue in sin and disobedience every day and still be righteous; for the righteousness and the obedience of Christ is imputed to them simply because they recognize him as the world's Savior. We must bear in mind, however, that the righteousness of God which Paul says is imputed to us covers only the ground of our "sins that are past"—those committed before we found Christ. From the moment of our justification we must ourselves live "in holiness and righteousness before him, all the days of our life" (Luke 1:75). Paul anticipated and repudiated this false conclusion regarding the imputing of Christ's righteousness to Christians, saying, "Shall we continue in sin, that grace may abound?" The very idea was repulsive to his mind, and he answered, "God forbid. How shall we that are dead to sin, live any longer therein?" (Rom. 6:1-2).

While justification signifies primarily a judicial acquittal, the opposite of condemnation, the primary meaning of Bible *conversion* is a change wrought in the individual himself.

So far as the term "conversion" itself is concerned, it signifies merely "a change from one state to another"; hence, it is often used for a mere outward reformation or a change of beliefs or doctrinal convictions. Bible conversion is more than this; it signifies a real change of heart and life. "Repent ye therefore, and be converted, that your sins may be blotted out, when the times of refreshing shall come from the presence of the Lord" (Acts 3:19). (See also Ps. 51:9-10, 13; Matt. 18:3.)

The experience of salvation received through Christ is also represented as a *new birth* of the Spirit. Jesus himself introduced this doctrine. "He came unto his own, and his own received him not. But as many as received him, to them gave he

power to become the sons of God, even to them that believe
on his name: which were born, not of blood, nor of the will
of the flesh, nor of the will of man, but of God" (John 1:11-
13). According to this text, all who during the incarnation received Christ and believed on his name were born of God.

So, too, when Nicodemus came by night to interview the
Savior, acknowledging him as a teacher come from God, "Jesus
answered and said unto him, Verily, verily I say unto thee,
Except a man be born again, he cannot see the kingdom of
God" (John 3:3). Nicodemus understood about natural birth,
but could not comprehend this idea of a second birth that even
an old man might experience. So Jesus explained: "That which
is born of the flesh is flesh; and that which is born of the
Spirit is spirit. Marvel not that I said unto thee, Ye must be
born again" (vss. 6-7).

The prominent idea connected with birth is a bringing into
life. In the Scriptures sinful man is represented as being in
a state of spiritual death. To know God and to be associated
with him in holiness and fellowship is life eternal, the normal
sphere of the soul's happiness (John 17:3). On the other hand,
to be cut off by sin and separated from that vital union with
our maker is spiritual death. "I was alive without the law
once: but when the commandment came, sin revived, and I
died" (Rom. 7:9). Isaiah 59:1-2 declares that sin separates
men from God. Paul says: "She that liveth in pleasure is dead
while she liveth" (I Tim. 5:6); "You, being dead in your sins"
(Col. 2:13); "You hath he quickened, who were dead in trespasses and sins; wherein in time past ye walked according
to the course of this world" (Eph. 2:1-2). (See also John 10:10;
5:24; I John 5:11-12.)

The new birth is an experience to be obtained now. "Whoso-
ever believeth that Jesus is the Christ is born of God" (I
John 5:1). "Behold, what manner of love the Father hath be-
stowed upon us, that we should be called the sons of God. . . .
Beloved, now are we the sons of God" (3:1-2). (See also I
John 3:9, 14; 2:29; 4:7; I Pet. 1:23; 2:2; Rom. 8:16.)

We must not overlook the miraculous feature of this new
birth, this bringing into life. In the natural world, life proceeds only from life. Things inanimate can never endow them-

selves with natural life. So it is also in the spiritual realm. Man, who is "dead in trespasses and in sins," can never endow himself with spiritual life. He may possibly reform himself in certain particulars and perform many good works, but after he has reached the end of all self-effort he will simply be a good moral man, and not what the Scriptures describe as a Christian; for a Christian is a good man *plus something else.* The additional something is life from God, which is infused by the divine Spirit into our hearts. "He that hath the Son hath life; and he that hath not the Son of God hath not life"; for "this life is in his Son" (I John 5:12, 11).

Knowledge of Salvation

This experience of salvation taught in the New Testament is not imaginary; it is a blessed reality. When presenting this subject the Apostles always spoke with certainty. John affirmed: "We know that we have passed from death unto life" (I John 3:14); "We know that we are of God" (5:19); "We are of God. . . . Every one that loveth is born of God, and knoweth God" (4:6-7).

Negatively, we are made conscious of this great change by the fact that all our sins are removed. It was the purpose of God "to give knowledge of salvation unto his people by the remission of their sins" (Luke 1:77). When the seeker, who is made deeply conscious of his sins and is heavily burdened with the load of his guilt, comes to Jesus, confesses and forsakes his sins according to the requirements of the Bible, the good Lord graciously sweeps them all away by the power of his grace. Then the sweet peace of heaven flows into the regenerated heart, and no one is needed to inform him that he is saved; for he is the first one to realize it. The experience of freedom from sin and its guilt is now as real as the fact of sin was. But this is not all. New feelings, new hopes, and new aspirations spring up in the soul, and he is made to realize the truth of Paul's words: "Therefore if any man be in Christ, he is a new creature: old things are passed away; behold, all things are become new. And all things are of God" (II Cor. 5:17-18).

Another clear evidence of our salvation is the radical change that is wrought in our affections. First, they become centered on God. While living a sinful life, men do not really love God from the heart, for they are living in rebellion or in a state of indifference toward the claims of God upon them. Some descend so deeply into sin that they even become "haters of God" (Rom. 1:30). When our souls become awakened to the reality of the great love that God has shown to us, the manifestation of divine affection in the death of our Lord for us wins back our wandering affections, and we are ready to exclaim with the Apostle, "We love him, because he first loved us" (I John 4:19). Then how natural it is to obey God! "If a man love me," says Jesus, "he will keep my words" (John 14:23).

Second, we experience a real change in our affections with reference to those who have been our enemies. Instead of the hatred and the bitterness that we have felt for them, we now experience a sense of love reaching out toward them, and we are able to obey the very words of Christ: "Love your enemies, bless them that curse you, do good to them that hate you, and pray for them which despitefully use you, and persecute you; that ye may be the children of your Father which is in heaven" (Matt. 5:44-45).

Third, our feelings toward God's people are also changed, and "we know that we have passed from death unto life, because we love the brethren" (I John 3:14). "By this we know that we love the children of God, when we love God, and keep his commandments" (5:2). "My little children, let us not love in word, neither in tongue; but in deed and in truth. And hereby we know that we are of the truth, and shall assure our hearts before him" (3:18-19). So great is our holy love toward all the children of God that Christ has said, "By this shall all men know that ye are my disciples, if ye have love one to another" (John 13:35).

The best and clearest evidence of our acceptance with God is the internal witness of his Spirit. Salvation is received by faith. Paul said to the jailer, "Believe on the Lord Jesus Christ, and thou shalt be saved." The Apostle John says, "He that believeth on the Son of God hath the witness in himself" (I John 5:10). There is no such thing as exercising saving faith in Christ without experiencing within the assurance of the Holy Spirit that we are now saved. This witnessing cannot be well explained in words, but, thank God, it can be experienced. "The Spirit itself beareth witness with our spirit, that we are the children of God" (Rom. 8:16).

Reader, are you conscious that your sins have been definitely canceled and that you are now in possession of the Christ-life? If not, then let me inform you that you are not born again, hence you are not a true Christian. You may be a good moral person, humanly speaking, bearing an excellent reputation among men and professing to be a Christian, but you are not a Christian when measured in the light of God's Word. "Except a man be born again, he cannot see the kingdom of God."

Chapter 8

A HOLY LIFE

In the preceding chapter we showed what constitutes real Bible conversion—what it means to be born of God. In this chapter we desire to show what the Bible teaches concerning the life of those who have been born of God. "We know that whosoever is born of God sinneth not; but he that is begotten of God keepeth himself, and that wicked one toucheth him not" (I John 5:18).

What Is Sin?

The Apostle John defines sin in these words: "Whosoever committeth sin transgresseth also the law: for sin is the transgression of the law" (I John 3:4). As we can more appropriately treat the subject of God's law in a subsequent chapter, it will not be necessary to enter into it in this place. Suffice it to say that the law by which our conduct will be judged, the transgression of which constitutes sin, is "the law of Christ" (Gal. 6:2). Jesus himself said, "He that rejecteth me, and receiveth not my words, hath one that judgeth him: the word that I have spoken, the same shall judge him in the last day" (John 12:48).

Since we shall be judged in the last day by the law of Christ, it is evident that it is the law of Christ that we are now held responsible to obey. But God is just; therefore our responsibility is limited to our available degree of enlightenment, there being in the New Testament no such thing as sin in total ignorance of God's requirements. "If ye were blind [spiritually], ye should have no sin" (John 9:41). "If I had not come and spoken unto them, they had not had sin" (15:22). "Sin is not imputed when there is no law" (Rom. 5:13). "For where no law is, there is no transgression" (4:15). We must possess some knowledge of our obligations, so that the will is involved; otherwise we are not reckoned transgressors. "Therefore to him that knoweth to do good, and doeth it not, to him it is sin" (Jas. 4:17). On this principle, to him that

49

knows that he should not do evil, and then does it, to him it is sin.

All Men Are Sinners

It is a fact that in all places and in all ages of the world men have acknowledged that they were under sin; for all realize that their wills have been involved in acts which they recognize to be in their very nature wrong. The Bible recognizes this universality of sin, "There is no man that sinneth not" (I Kings 8:46). (See also Rom. 3:23; Gal. 3:22.)

But while the Old Testament recognizes the universal prevalence of sin, it also contains predictions of a divine provision for its removal. Isaiah, speaking of Christ, said, "He will come and save you" (35:4). (See also Dan. 9:24; Matt. 1:21.)

Christians Are Saved from Sin

"And ye know that he was manifested to take away our sins; and in him is no sin. Whosoever abideth in him sinneth not: whosoever sinneth hath not seen him, neither known him" (I John 3:5-6). This is the uniform gospel standard, as we shall see.

Christ taught that Christians are saved from sin. "Verily, verily I say unto you, Whosoever committeth sin is the servant of sin. . . . If the Son therefore shall make you free, ye shall be free indeed" (John 8:34-36). Here is promised a perfect freedom from the bondage of sin.

In the fifth chapter of John we read of a certain impotent man lying at the pool of Bethesda, whose infirmity was of thirty-eight years' duration. Jesus came along and healed him. "Afterward Jesus findeth him in the temple, and said unto him, Behold, thou art made whole: sin no more, lest a worse thing come unto thee" (vs. 14). Now it is preposterous to suppose that Christ was unjust and that he would give a commandment that could not be obeyed—a commandment whose violation would bring upon the poor man a sorer affliction than he had endured during those thirty-eight long years. Christ's command could be obeyed. This man received power from the Lord to go and live free from sin. (See also John 8:3-11.)

Peter taught the same. "Repent ye therefore, and be converted, that your sins may be blotted out, when the times of refreshing shall come from the presence of the Lord" (Acts 3:19). "Christ also suffered for us, leaving us an example, that ye should follow his steps: who did no sin, neither was guile found in his mouth" (I Pet. 2:21-22).

The teaching of Paul is the same. "Awake to righteousness, and sin not; for some have not the knowledge of God: I speak this to your shame" (I Cor. 15:34). Almost the whole of Romans 6 is devoted to the subject of the Christian's deliverance from sin. I will quote just a few verses wherein it is stated. "What shall we say then? shall we continue in sin, that grace may abound? God forbid. How shall we that are dead to sin, live any longer therein?" (vss. 1-2). "Likewise reckon ye also yourselves to be dead indeed unto sin, but alive unto God through Jesus Christ our Lord. Let not sin therefore reign in your mortal body, that ye should obey it in the lusts thereof" (vss. 11-12). "Sin shall not have dominion over you: for ye are not under the law, but under grace" (vs. 14). (See also vss. 17-18, 22.)

Some people attempt to prove that Paul himself was a sinner and a defender of sin; but this chapter alone is sufficient to forever settle his attitude *as a Christian* toward the subject of sin. This point we shall refer to again in the present chapter.

John also says the same. "If we walk in the light, as he is in the light, we have fellowship one with another, and the blood of Jesus Christ his Son cleanseth us from all sin. If we say that we have no sin [to be cleansed from], we deceive ourselves, and the truth is not in us. If we confess our sins, he is faithful and just to forgive us our sins, and to cleanse us from all unrighteousness" (I John 1:7-9). Here a perfect cleansing from sin is taught, upon condition that we do not cover our sins up and deny them, but "walk in the light" and "confess our sins." The same writer also shows that we must live before Christ in this holy state. (See also 2:6.) How did Christ walk? Peter tells us that he "did no sin, neither was guile found in his mouth" (I Pet. 2:22). Hence we must do no sin. This is the Christian standard.

John writes again, "My little children, these things write I

unto you, that ye sin not" (I John 2:1). In the same verse he
goes on to show that "if any man sin, we have an advocate with
the Father, Jesus Christ the righteous." This, however, does
not in the least weaken the standard here set forth in verse 6.
The Apostle goes a step further; he shows that Christians not
only "ought" to walk this way, but that they really *do*. "Whosoever abideth in him sinneth not: whosoever sinneth hath not
seen him, neither known him" (3:6). "We know that whosoever is born of God sinneth not; but he that is begotten of God
keepeth himself, and that wicked one toucheth him not" (5:18).

"Little children, let no man deceive you: he that doeth righteousness is righteous, even as he is righteous. . . . Whosoever
is born of God doth not commit sin; for his seed remaineth in
him: and he cannot sin, because he is born of God" (I John
3:7-9). Reader, mark this fact: John does not say that God's
people confess their sins every day or repent of them frequently; he says that they "do not commit sin." Thousands of
professed Christians have asked the question, "Who are those
'just persons, which need no repentance,' of whom Christ
speaks?" (Luke 15:7). The answer is very clear: They are the
Christians, those who have been born of God; for "whosoever
is born of God doth not commit sin." They need not, and hence
could not, repent.

God draws a distinct line of demarcation between sinners
and Christians. We have already shown by many texts that
God's people are saved from their sins.

Now we shall notice what the New Testament has to say,
by way of contrast, concerning the other class.

Jesus: "Whosoever committeth sin is the servant of sin"
(John 8:34).

Paul: "When ye were the servants of sin, ye were free from
righteousness" (Rom. 6:20).

Peter: "Having eyes full of adultery, and that cannot cease
from sin. . . . To whom the mist of darkness is reserved forever" (II Pet. 2:14-17).

James: "Ye adulterers and adulteresses, know ye not that the
friendship of the world is enmity with God? whosoever therefore will be a friend of the world is the enemy of God" (Jas.
4:4).

Jude: "Ungodly sinners . . . walking after their own lusts . . . having men's persons in admiration because of advantage. . . . These be they who separate themselves [from the truth and from the doctrine of a sinless life], sensual, having not the Spirit" (Jude 15-16, 19).

John: "We know that we are of God, and the whole world lieth in wickedness" (I John 5:19). "Whosoever sinneth hath not seen him [Christ], neither known him" (3:6). Mark this contrast: "He that committeth sin is of the devil; for the devil sinneth from the beginning. . . . Whosoever is born of God doth not commit sin; . . . In this the children of God are manifest, and the children of the devil: whosoever doeth not righteousness is not of God" (vss. 8-10), and "he that doeth righteousness, is righteous, even as he [Christ] is righteous" (vs. 7). The line of distinction which God has made is drawn between those who commit sin and those who do not commit sin. Those who do not sin are born of God, and know God, and have his righteousness; on the other hand, those who commit sin are the servants of sin and are doing the devil's work, hence they belong to him—are "of the devil"—and are not the children of God at all.

Some Objections Answered

Objection 1. "There is no man that sinneth not" (I Kings 8:46). "For there is not a just man upon earth, that doeth good, and sinneth not" (Eccles. 7:20).

Answer. These words were uttered by King Solomon, who lived about one thousand years before Christ, in the dispensation when it was "not possible that the blood of bulls and of goats should take away sins" (Heb. 10:4). Many men of that dispensation possessed great faith in God and, considering the general standards of those times, lived very good lives; hence they were accepted by God on the ground of their faith when they conformed to the highest standard of his revealed will.

But the experience of the new birth, the regeneration of the soul which makes men "new creatures," was not realized in those days, and people then did not claim to live without committing sin. The plan of salvation from all sin through Christ was from the foundation of the world a "mystery" which was "hid in God" (Eph. 3:9). Jesus said to his disciples: "Many prophets and righteous men [of the old dispensation] have desired to see those things which ye see, and have not seen them; and to hear those things which ye hear, and have not heard them." "Blessed are your eyes, for they see: and your ears, for they hear" (Matt. 13:17, 16).

These prophets, however, caught a glimpse of this coming redemption, and wrote of it, though they did not themselves experience it. This is clearly stated in I Peter 1:9-12. This makes it clear that the experience of salvation which we now receive through Christ was not experienced before his coming, even by the prophets who wrote of it. The same argument explains Ecclesiastes 7:20, which was written under the old dispensation.

Objection 2. Paul's experience in Romans 7, where he says: "I know that in me . . . dwelleth no good thing: for to will is present with me; but how to perform that which is good I find not. For the good that I would I do not: but the evil which I would not, that I do. Now if I do that I would not, it is no more I that do it, but sin that dwelleth in me. I find then a law, that, when I would do good, evil is present with me. . . . O wretched man that I am!" (vss. 18-21, 24).

Answer. A study of the entire chapter shows clearly that the Apostle was describing his experience under the Law of Moses, before he found Christ. He first speaks of his infantile state when he was "alive without the law"—did not even know that the Law said, "Thou shalt not covet." Afterward "when the commandment came" to him, he says, "sin revived, and I died." (7:7, 9.)

This sin experience was the experience of Saul, the man who zealously defended the Law and persecuted the church of God. Immediately following we have, in his own words, the experience of Paul the Christian: "There is therefore now no condemnation to them which are in Christ Jesus, who walk not after the flesh, but after the Spirit. For the law of the Spirit of life in Christ Jesus hath made me free from the law of sin and death. For what the law [of Moses] could not do, in that it was weak through the flesh, God sending his own Son in the likeness of sinful flesh, and for sin, condemned sin

in the flesh: that the righteousness of the law might be fulfilled in us, who walk not after the flesh, but after the Spirit"
(Rom. 8:1-4).

Reader, which do you desire, the experience of Saul or the
experience of Paul? After he found deliverance from sin
through Christ, he taught that Christians are to live without
sin. "Shall we continue in sin, that grace may abound? God
forbid. How shall we that are dead to sin live any longer therein?" (Rom. 6:1-2). "For sin shall not have dominion over
you: for ye are not under the law, but under grace" (vs. 14).
This last text clears up the entire matter. Under the Law, sin
had dominion over the people; under grace, God's people have
dominion over sin. Under the Law, it might be said, "There is
not a just man upon earth, that doeth good, and sinneth not";
but under grace "whosoever is born of God doth not commit
sin."

That the sin experience described in Romans 7 was not the
experience of Paul the Christian at the time when he was
writing this chapter is shown also by other testimonies of Paul.
(See I Thess. 2:10; Acts 23:1; 24:16; II Tim. 4:7.)

Objections based on certain other texts of Scripture (for
example, Romans 3:10) are of this same general character;
for almost without exception they relate to Old Testament
conditions, not to the New Testament standard of salvation.

The doctrine of sinning Christians originates in a perverse
state of the soul, in an incorrect definition of sin, or else in a
failure to understand dispensational truth. A proper understanding of the difference between the old covenant and the
new will forever settle the question of the present relation of
God's people to sin.

Freedom from Worldliness

Worldliness is simply another division of the subject of sin,
for worldliness is sin. However, there are some special thoughts
that I wish to present under this heading.

Since sin in its various forms has become universal, surrounding us on all sides as really as nature itself, the Bible
writers often refer to it as "the world." This expression includes not only the grosser forms of sin but all manner of dis-

obedience to God of whatever nature or extent. God's people must be free from all these things. Paul wrote to the brethren who had been quickened in Christ, "In time past ye walked according to the course of this world" (Eph. 2:2). But Christ "gave himself for our sins, that he might deliver us from this present evil world" (Gal. 1:4).

That our separation from the world in this sense is to be real is shown by the words of Christ, "If ye were of the world, the world would love his own: but because ye are not of the world, but I have chosen you out of the world, therefore the world hateth you" (John 15:19). Reader, bear in mind that if you take your stand for God and for the whole truth of his Word, determined to be free from all worldliness, there will be real separation in spirit and in life between you and the world. You will even have opposition. "Yea, and all that will live godly in Christ Jesus shall suffer persecution" (II Tim. 3:12).

We have the testimony of Jesus himself that the first disciples were free from the world. To us this certainly means that everything that partakes of the spirit and nature of the sinful world must be forsaken—worldly amusements, worldly associates, worldly ambitions, worldly sentiments, and worldly attire—everything that is not in strict harmony with the teaching of God's Word. "Love not the world, neither the things that are in the world. If any man love the world, the love of the Father is not in him. For all that is in the world, the lust of the flesh, and the lust of the eyes, and the pride of life, is not of the Father, but is of the world. And the world passeth away, and the lust thereof; but he that doeth the will of God abideth forever" (I John 2:15-17).

According to the principles of truth already shown, it is evident that the holy people of God cannot go to and participate in those amusements whose direct object is to cater to foolishness, vanity, and sin. At the present day Satan is seeking by this means to draw the hearts of the people away from righteousness and into questionable ways of pleasure and sin, thus causing them to forget and forsake God. Especially is this true respecting the young. How many forms of worldly amusement have been devised to serve this purpose! These things "are not of the Father, but are of the world"; and no true child of God can indulge in such things without loss to his spirituality, injury to his influence as a Christian, and, if the indulgence is continued, the final loss of his soul. "Flee also youthful lusts: but follow righteousness, faith, charity, peace, with them that call on the Lord out of a pure heart" (II Tim. 2:22).

The true and faithful Christian must live a life of prayer and devotion to God. By this means he is refreshed from day to day and he obtains conquering grace for trials and temptations. This life of devotion cannot exist where the spirit of worldliness is allowed sway. Those who attend or participate in sinful amusements soon feel no burden for secret prayer and devotion, and they have little or no active interest in the salvation of souls; on the other hand, those who seek to be spiritual and to live in prayer before God have no desire for such amusements. They are dead to the world and its pleasures. Of them Jesus can say, "They are not of the world, even as I am not of the world."

If we as the people of God have holy, humble hearts, hearts free from vanity and pride, then even our outward lives should in every way be consistent with the inward condition. The Word of God says, "Glorify God in your body, and in your spirit, which are God's" (I Cor. 6:20). We must "be holy both in body and in spirit" (7:34). When people's hearts are full of the "pride of life" they manifest it outwardly by proud actions, extravagances in personal attire, and in worldly adornments. Does the Scripture have any pronouncement on this subject?

"Whose adorning let it not be that outward adorning of plaiting the hair, and of wearing of gold, or of putting on of apparel; but let it be the hidden man of the heart, in that which is not corruptible, even the ornament of a meek and quiet spirit, which is in the sight of God of great price" (I Pet. 3:3-4).

To some sincere Christian people the first part of the foregoing is regarded as the language of absolute prohibition. Such an interpretation can apparently be maintained so far as the "wearing of gold" for adornment is concerned, but it becomes rather difficult with respect to "plaiting the hair" and the "putting on of apparel"; for a woman who has "long hair," which Paul in another place says "is a glory to her" (I Cor. 11:15), must of necessity do something to care for her hair properly, and everyone must necessarily put on personal wearing apparel of some kind. Is the language of this text intended to signify absolute prohibition, or is it not, rather, simply the language of comparison, with a view to proper emphasis?

It is our desire to present what the Bible actually means to teach, not to see if it can be made to sanction what may be extreme or unwarranted views. We do know that the Bible frequently employs language that is apparently prohibitive in character even when the context itself or other plain passages show that it is only meant to be *comparative*—used in order to place proper emphasis on the greater of the two things contrasted. For example, in Matthew 6:19-20 Jesus said, "Lay not up for yourselves treasures upon earth . . . but lay up for yourselves treasures in heaven." Is that text designed to prohibit all ownership of material things? The Corinthian brethren had "houses to eat and to drink in" (I Cor. 11:22), and Paul evidently admits that some Christians in his day were even rich; for he says, "Charge them that are rich in this world, that they be not high-minded, nor trust in uncertain riches, but in the living God" (I Tim. 6:17).

Even if we concede that the language of I Peter 3:3-4 is comparative only, designed to throw particular emphasis on the inner "ornament of a meek and quiet spirit," we must acknowledge that in I Timothy 2:9-10 Paul makes a strong, direct reference to *outward* adornment: "In like manner also, that women adorn themselves in modest apparel, with shamefacedness and sobriety; not with braided hair, or gold, or pearls, or costly array; but (which becometh women professing godliness) with good works." This text certainly implies that the extreme type of outward personal adornment to which Paul refers and names outright does not constitute "modest apparel," and that it does not become "women professing godliness." The actual standard of the Christian's dress given here is "modest apparel." This is rather a relative term, it is true, but whatever its adaptation to the established customs of society may be, it is evident that it excludes and prohibits whatever ranks as immodest styles, flippant fashions, and the lavish personal ornamentations of proud and worldly-minded people. "Modest apparel" may be defined as the middle ground between two extremes. To those of careless, slovenly habits it would mean to clean up and dress up; to those of the fashionable, gaudy type, decorated with useless, showy ornaments, such as the "gold, pearls, and costly array" mentioned in this text, it could mean nothing less than a trimming down, a discarding of that which naturally ministers to and suggests pride and worldly-mindedness. Then both these classes, and all classes, may walk on the highway of holiness together as exemplary Christians, exhibiting consistently the meekness and humility of Christ.

"Modest apparel" is the ordinary, regular standard of dress fixed by common custom and expected of everyone by right-thinking people. This is such a standard as holy, humble, Spirit-led people of God would naturally accept even if there were no texts in the Bible bearing on the subject. Real Christians, who are eager to please God and to show forth his praises, wish to "abstain from all appearance of evil" (I Thess. 5:22). Such a Christian does not seek to behave or to dress in such an extreme way as to be easily mistaken for one of that proud, haughty, graceless class of superficially adorned worldlings who are strangers to God and to his blessed Word. Real Christians *belong to another class*—they desire to be "an example of the believers" (I Tim. 4:12).

Nor is holy life to be judged solely by a negative standard—by what of sin and worldliness we put off. There is a positive side. When we die to the world, we "put on Christ." Then we can say with Paul, "I am crucified with Christ: nevertheless I live; yet not I, but Christ liveth in me: and the life which I now live in the flesh, I live by the faith of the Son of God, who loved me, and gave himself for me" (Gal. 2:20). Our whole desire is to manifest Christ to the world. Being "risen with Christ," we "seek those things which are above" (Col. 3:1). We "put on therefore, as the elect of God, holy and beloved, bowels of mercies, kindness, humbleness of mind, meekness, long-suffering" (vs. 12). The graces of the Spirit implanted within find outward expression in "the fruit of the Spirit," which is "love, joy, peace, long-suffering, gentleness, goodness, faith, meekness, temperance" (Gal. 5:22-23). Our aim in life is to have always a conscience void of offense toward God and toward man. However, we do not allow the voice of conscience alone to dictate in matters of religious faith, but we render loving and willing obedience to all the commandments of our Lord and require our conscience to come into line with what he plainly says. Thus, our lives are free and happy and are made a blessing to all around us. This phase of the subject will be treated more fully later.

Oh, how much it means to serve God "without fear, in holiness and righteousness before him, all the days of our life"! (Luke 1:74-75).

Christian Stewardship

The personal experience of freedom from sin and true holiness of heart really implies, as a fundamental concept, the idea of an actual stewardship of life. Since we are bought with a great price, we are no longer our own. And if it is really true that we are not our own we should easily recognize and accept the standard of the apostolic church as expressed in the words, "Neither said any of them that ought of the things which he possessed was his own" (Acts 4:32).

The stewardship obligation is based on the sovereign ownership of God. He created all things, hence all things rightfully belong to him for his own use and purpose. Man, the creature, may be entrusted by God with certain rights and possessions, but man is not sovereign owner of anything. The general teaching of the Bible throughout shows that man is under constant obligation to God and that God expects man to acknowledge this stewardship relation. This obligation is not merely an arbitrary arrangement or requirement, but it exists in the nature of things, prior to all enacted legislation pertaining thereto.

The earliest historic example of man's voluntary response to this basic principle of right is found in the family of Adam, when, as a definite part of their worship and service to God, Cain and Abel brought material offerings to the Lord (Gen. 4:3-5). The first time the material phase of that natural obligation is expressed in terms of one-tenth is found in Genesis 14:18-20, when Abraham gave "tithes of all" to Melchizedek, king of Salem, "priest of the most high God." In the New Testament dispensation we find this particular tithing example given prominent consideration and sanction by apostolic authority in the Book of Hebrews (7:1-9).

The tithe was regarded as due to the Lord. Jacob, following the example of Abraham, vowed to the Lord, "Of all that thou shalt give me I will surely give the tenth unto thee" (Gen. 28:22).

Later, when the Law of Moses was given, tithing, supplemented from time to time by freewill offerings, was incorporated into the legal system with considerable detail as to the manner in which it was to be carried out. But it was clearly shown to be the Lord's due. "And all the tithe of the land, whether of the seed of the land, or of the fruit of the tree, is the Lord's: it is holy unto the Lord" (Lev. 27:30).

Stewardship as exemplified in the Old Testament included not only offerings of material possessions, but *time* also. Every seventh day was a Sabbath of rest, and there were also other solemn festivals and holy days. God made a very real claim upon the time of the Israelites.

In the New Testament the old-time Sabbath appears to be regarded as typical in its nature. (See chapter 22, under subhead "New Testament Ceremonies.")

As to stewardship in its relation to material possessions, Christ evidently sanctioned the tithing system, even while condemning certain scribes, Pharisees, and hypocrites because they had exalted it above moral and spiritual duties and obligations. "Ye pay tithe of mint and anise and cummin, and have omitted the weightier matters of the law, judgment, mercy, and faith: these ought ye to have done, and not to leave the other undone" (Matt. 23:23).

The Apostle Paul says, "As I have given order to the churches of Galatia, even so do ye. Upon the first day of the week let every one of you lay by him in store, as God hath prospered him" (I Cor. 16:1-2). While this particular text does not specify tithing as such, it does imply the same basic idea of stewardship, because it expects of "every one of you" a proportionate surrender of earned income—"as God hath prospered him"—on the first day of the week, the time of the regularly recurring religious services.

While tithing was incorporated into the Mosaic law system, as we have noted, it did not originate with that system; hence it did not necessarily cease with it. The fundamental law of stewardship relations existing between the creature and the Creator—the principle of honoring God with our substance—knows no dispensational change. That tithing, divinely approved from the earliest ages, automatically carries over into the new dispensation may at least be inferred from the fact that the New Testament provides no other regular system of financial support for God's work.

In practical experience in our own day those congregations which have voluntarily accepted the tithing plan, supplemented at times by freewill offerings for various special projects or causes, have prospered. On the other hand, congregations that have shunned the tithing system on account of its former association with the Mosaic law have been forced by their own program to resort to frequent financial drives and to various sorts of schemes and devices for raising money, much to the detriment of the church itself and to its influence in the community. It is certain that God did approve tithing at one time; but where has he ever put his sanction on this complicated modern technique created by men for the purpose of getting money?

If we will but recognize the principle of stewardship of possessions—that we owe something to God regularly, according to our earned income—we shall experience in our individual lives today the fulfillment of the promise of old: "Bring ye all the tithes into the storehouse . . . and prove me now herewith, saith the Lord of hosts, if I will not open you the windows of heaven, and pour you out a blessing, that there shall not be room enough to receive it" (Mal. 3:10).

Chapter 9

SANCTIFICATION AS A BIBLE DOCTRINE

Conversion and a subsequent life of holiness are indeed a high state of grace. Nevertheless, it is not the complete sum of Christian experience as set forth in the New Testament. As my object is to set forth the true Bible standard, I shall proceed to show that the New Testament clearly teaches a second, definite work of divine grace wrought in the heart by the Holy Spirit—holiness perfected, or entire sanctification. The Bible writers speak of it from various standpoints, sometimes emphasizing one phase of the subject and sometimes another and therefore using a variety of terms. All these, however, are resolved into the same thing. When the subject is considered from the standpoint of entire sanctification, a result is thereby expressed, and the cause of this result may or may not be stated in a given instance. We shall consider sanctification first as a result, or work in the soul, and then proceed to show the cause that produces this effect.

The Apostle Paul states that God hath "chosen you to salvation through sanctification of the Spirit and belief of the truth" (II Thess. 2:13). Sanctification is therefore a part of the work of salvation and belongs to all God's people. Christ prayed earnestly that his disciples might have this experience, as we read in John 17:17. He did even more than pray for it; he gave his life that it might be accomplished (Heb. 13:12). But it is his own people that are to be sanctified; for Paul informs us that "Christ also loved the church, and gave himself for it; that he might sanctify and cleanse it" (Eph. 5:25-26). (See also I Thess. 5:23-24; II Tim. 2:21.)

This doctrine was also taught by Peter who states that our election is "through sanctification of the Spirit" (I Pet. 1:2). These texts, and others that might be cited, show clearly that sanctification is a New Testament doctrine.

What Does Sanctification Signify?

Sanctification signifies two distinct things: first, a consecrating, or setting apart to a holy or religious use—a legal or ceremonial holiness; second, a definite cleansing and purifying of the heart and affections of men—a moral work.

Now, the term is used in the Bible with both of these significations; therefore we must be careful to "rightly divide the word of truth." In the Old Testament, under the law dispensation, sanctification is often mentioned, but it was merely a legal sanctification, or a setting apart to a religious use. This was before the time when full salvation could be wrought in the soul through the blood of Christ, and a moral change was not under consideration; in fact, the objects of that sanctification were in many cases wholly incapable of receiving any moral change, for inanimate objects, as well as animate, received it.

In the New Testament the term "sanctification" includes the other signification—a purging or cleansing of the moral nature of man. We must observe, however, that according to the definition already given, and according to its use in the Bible, "sanctification" applies to all religious consecration and to all moral cleansing, irrespective of degree. Christ referred to the brazen altar—the altar upon which gifts and offerings were placed—when he declared that it "sanctifieth the gift" (Matt. 23:19).

The term "sanctification," in its broad sense, covers the whole of the Christian experience, irrespective of degree, and is thus used without distinction in many texts. However, the term is also used in a specific sense, referring to a second work of divine grace wrought in the heart of the Christian believer —a work known as holiness perfected, or entire sanctification. "And the very God of peace sanctify you wholly [entirely]" (I Thess. 5:23). It is in this latter sense that I shall now employ the term. Therefore, specifically, sanctification is

For Justified People Only

None but human beings can receive this glorious experience of sanctification, and not all of them obtain it; for it is reserved for those who have already been justified from their actual transgressions through the blood of Jesus Christ. In other words, people must be genuinely converted to God, born again, and living the holy life required by the New Testament before they are scriptural candidates for entire sanctification. In Christ's prayer for his disciples, he said, "I pray for them: I pray not for the world, but for them which thou hast given me. . . . Sanctify them" (John 17:9, 17). (See also Eph. 5:25-26.) People must first "receive forgiveness of sins" before they can obtain the "inheritance among them which are sanctified" (Acts 26:18). It was to the brethren at Thessalonica, to those who were "in God the Father and in the Lord Jesus Christ" (I Thess. 1:1), that Paul wrote when he said, "The very God of peace sanctify you wholly" (5:23).

From these scriptural statements it will be seen that sanctification is

A Second Work of Grace

There is a definite reason for this twofoldness in the redemption of the individual believer. Sin exists in two forms—actual and inherent; that is, there is a disposition to wrong received through natural generation, and there are willful acts of wrong which we commit after reaching the age when we have a knowledge of right and wrong. "Native depravity" properly expresses the first form and "transgression" or "sin" the second; but since theologians usually term the evil tendencies of human nature "Adamic sin," or "original sin," I shall adopt that terminology and speak of sin in two forms—inherent and actual. We are in no sense individually responsible for possessing the evil nature that we inherit; but we are wholly responsible for our own sinful acts committed later. Repentance can apply only to our own individual acts of wrong; hence forgiveness and conversion are of necessity limited to that aspect, as we shall soon see by the teaching of the Scriptures. Therefore, any attempt to identify in redemption these two distinct forms of sin is a mistake.

We have no need of proving that men are guilty of actual transgressions; the fact is well known and acknowledged. However, the Scriptures assert that "all have sinned, and come short of the glory of God" (Rom. 3:23). Concerning inherent sin, we must give the more exact statements of the Scriptures; for although it is generally admitted, it is sometimes denied.

"The wicked are estranged from the womb: they go astray as soon as they be born, speaking lies" (Ps. 58:3). While the psalmist is here simply describing a fact, the verse contains at least a strong intimation of an inward bent to evil. Again, he says, "Behold, I was shapen in iniquity; and in sin did my mother conceive me" (51:5). This text shows that an evil disposition is a part of man from the earliest moment of his existence. And the Apostle Paul distinctly affirms that we are all "by nature the children of wrath" (Eph. 2:3).

In relating his own experience, Paul gives a clear description of sin in these two forms (Rom. 7:7-13). Here the Apostle speaks first of his experience as an infant, when he had no knowledge of God's law, did not even know that it said, "Thou shalt not covet." At this time, although he was "alive without the law," he had in him something that he calls sin, but "without the law sin was dead." Later, "when the commandment came" to his understanding, and he transgressed it, then, he says, "sin revived, and I died"—he became "dead in trespasses and sins" (Eph. 2:1). How clear this twofoldness of sin! And this has been the experience of all who have reached the age of moral responsibility.

Our foreparents were created "in righteousness and true holiness," but from this lofty estate they fell, thereby plunging the world into the darkness of sin; for as a result all have received an evil nature, as we have already shown. From this fact it is evident that when we are born into the world, though we are perfectly innocent, we are *one degree below* the line of perfect holiness, since we possess the nature of sin. When we reach the age of moral responsibility and take upon ourselves a sinful life, we fall *another degree lower,* so that we are now *two steps* below the original plane of holiness.

Now the design of Christ is to restore mankind in salvation to the high plane from which they fell; and since they have descended two degrees into sin, there must of necessity be two steps upward in redemption. Are there not the same number of steps in a stairway when a person ascends as when he descends? And the last step taken coming down will be the first one to take going up. So in redemption. The last step in the descent was our willful departure from God into actual sins, so our first step in salvation is *willingly* to return to God, leaving behind all the sins that we have committed (Isa. 55: 7; 1: 18). "If we confess our sins, he is faithful and just to forgive us our sins, and to cleanse us from all unrighteousness" (I John 1: 9). This confession and pardon relate solely to our own sinful acts, and this is what Peter terms conversion: "Repent ye therefore, and be converted, that your sins may be blotted out" (Acts 3: 19).

Jesus teaches that the converted man is like a little child once more (Matt. 18: 3). While this language doubtless refers directly to the humility and innocence of childhood, it certainly implies a moral restoration of the individual. In other words, the person whose individual sins have been confessed, forgiven, and blotted out is "converted" and has regained the moral condition of innocency from which he departed at the age of accountability (Rom. 7: 9). But as the infant is one degree below the plane of perfect holiness, so also is the converted person. He is even called a "babe" (I Pet. 2: 2; Heb. 5: 13) and is exhorted to go on unto perfection, "perfecting holiness in the fear of God" (II Cor. 7:1); he is informed by the Bible that so far as moral purity is concerned God hath "perfected forever them that are sanctified" (Heb. 10: 14).

The Apostle John, in that epistle in which he speaks so often about being born of God, teaches most clearly that these "sons of God" still stand in need of purification. (See I John 3:2-3.) Again I call attention to Paul's words, "Christ also loved the church, and gave himself for it; that he might sanctify and cleanse it" (Eph. 5: 25-26).

Furthermore, this need of cleansing can be tested in the experience of the Apostles themselves. In John 1: 12-13 we read that those who received Christ during his incarnation and believed on his name became sons of God by being born of God. Christ said to the seventy disciples, "Your names are written in heaven" (Luke 10: 20). Yet we have in the gospel narrative clear evidences that these apostles still possessed the nature of evil, as when the ten were "moved with indignation" against the two who sought positions of authority over the others. (See Matt. 20:20-24; Mark 9:34.) Since, therefore, they needed a cleansing from this inbred sin, Christ prayed to the Father, "Sanctify them" (John 17:17).

This twofoldness of salvation work is also shown under the figure of a vine and its branches (John 15:1-2. 5). The individual Christian is a branch of the true vine—Christ. If he ceases to bear the fruit of the Spirit, he is taken away; but if he is a fruitful branch, he is to be *purged,* so that he can bring forth more fruit.

The promise of a second work was given to the Apostles in a threefold form:

1. The purging already mentioned.

2. "I will pray the Father, and he shall give you another Comforter, that he may abide with you forever; even the Spirit of truth; whom the world cannot receive, because it seeth him not, neither knoweth him: but ye know him; for he dwelleth with you, and shall be in you" (John 14:16-17).

3. In his prayer recorded in John 17, Jesus did not say a word about the Father's giving the Holy Spirit to the Apostles, but he did say, "Sanctify them through thy truth: thy word is truth" (vs. 17).

Now, his threefold promise is gathered up in one experience to be received by them, the Holy Spirit being *cause,* and purging, or sanctification, being the *result.* "Being sanctified by the Holy Ghost" (Rom. 15:16). So Christ's asking the Father to sanctify the Apostles was virtually asking him to give them the Holy Spirit; for when the Holy Spirit was received as their Comforter they were sanctified—"sanctified by the Holy Ghost."

So also the purging promised is the same, being the work of the Holy Ghost when received. "And God, which knoweth the hearts, bare them witness, giving them the Holy Ghost, even as he did unto us; and put no difference between us and them, purifying their hearts by faith" (Acts 15:8-9). This text refers to the time when the household of Cornelius were baptized with the Holy Spirit (chap. 10). So it is a scriptural fact that there is a purging of the heart, or entire sanctification, to be received subsequently to regeneration, and that it is obtained when the Holy Ghost is received as the abiding Comforter. Sin is twofold and salvation also is twofold. "He saved us, by the washing of regeneration, and renewing of the Holy Ghost; which he shed on us abundantly" (Titus 3:5-6).

The twofold aspect of salvation was typified by the tabernacle of the Mosaic dispensation. This ancient structure, the dwelling place of God on earth, consisted of two apartments surrounded by a court. In the court, directly in front of the entrance to the first apartment, stood the brazen altar, or altar of burnt offerings, and a laver containing water. The first apartment, which was entered from the court and was termed the "holy place," contained a table of showbread, a candlestick, and the golden altar, which stood just before the entrance into the second apartment. This second, or inner, apartment was called the "holy of holies," or "holiest of all." It contained the ark of the covenant, wherein were deposited the stone tables of the law.

The two apartments in the type must have their counterpart in the antitype. In the tabernacle there were two altars, as already observed, and the blood of sin offerings was *placed on both altars* (Lev. 4:7), thus clearly typifying *twofold cleansing.* For a full discussion of the two works as symbolized by the tabernacle, see pages 124-126 of the large edition.

Conditions for Sanctification

This blessed state of perfected holiness cannot be entered by sinners. The Holy Ghost is given, not to the world, but to those who are chosen out of the world—to those who are God's believing and obedient children. Therefore the first essential is that the candidate for sanctification possess a clear, definite experience of Bible justification, but this is not all.

It is in our effort to live a holy life that we are made painfully conscious of the presence of that evil nature within. Realizing that while the soul is fighting the devil on the outside there is also "a foe in the temple not subject to God," one cries out for an experience of heart purity. The first disciples were earnestly praying when they received this experience (Acts 1:14; 2:1-4). So was Cornelius when the way was opened for him to receive the Holy Ghost (10:2-3). Without strong desire and earnest prayer one will never obtain this definite work of grace.

The seeker must make a complete surrender to the whole will of God, a perfect consecration of time, talents, and all to His service, and of himself to be sacredly the Lord's for time and for eternity (Rom. 12:1-2). When this perfect consecration is made, God will be pleased to send his Holy Spirit in sanctifying power, purging the heart from the very nature of sin, and will himself take up his abode in the pure and devoted soul.

The Holy Ghost Baptism

The baptism of the Holy Ghost taught in the New Testament is a special endowment of the Spirit of God in the hearts of his believing and obedient children. Different expressions are used to convey this idea—baptism of the Holy Ghost (Matt. 3:11); the Holy Ghost given (John 7:39); receiving "the Spirit of truth" (14:17; 16:13); "Comforter" (14:16, 26; 15:26); receiving the Holy Ghost (20:22; Acts 8:17; 10:47); "filled with the Holy Ghost" (2:4; 4:31); "gift of the Holy Ghost" (2:38); the Spirit poured out upon men (2:17; 10:45). These expressions all refer to one and the same thing, as will be shown later. They simply represent different aspects of the one subject, just as the different expressions used for the first work of grace convey various shades of meaning, though meaning essentially the same thing.

The Work of the Holy Spirit

The work of the Holy Ghost in the heart of the believer who receives him is twofold—negative and positive. His negative work, as we have already shown, is to purify, or sanctify (Acts 15:8-9). The reception of the Spirit is compared to fire— "Baptize you with the Holy Ghost and with fire" (Matt. 3:11) —fire being a destructive and purifying element; and those who have thus been "sanctified by the Holy Ghost" are "pure in heart" (5:8), for he "hath perfected forever them that are sanctified. Whereof the Holy Ghost also is a witness" (Heb. 10:14-15). No element of impurity remains in the moral nature of one who has received the Holy Ghost: he is in this respect "perfected forever." Praise God for heart purity!

The positive work of the Holy Spirit is: (1) to give power — (Acts 1:8), (2) to guide (John 16:13), (3) to comfort (14:16-18, 4) to teach (14:26), (5) to increase spiritual fruits (15:2 with Gal. 5:22-23), (6) to unify God's people (John 17:20-23 with Acts 4:31-32), (7) to fit for service (Luke 24:49; II Tim. 2:21).

The baptism and work of the Holy Spirit are of great importance, both to the individual believer and to the work of God. To the individual it is the perfecting grace, "the grace wherein we stand" (Rom. 5:2); therefore, it completes our moral preparation for heaven. "Blessed are the pure in heart: for they shall see God" (Matt. 5:8).

As to the work of God, this divine experience is necessary in order properly to fit us for the Lord's service. Christ commanded his apostles to tarry in the city of Jerusalem until they were "endued with power from on high" (Luke 24:49; Acts 1:8). Paul teaches that by being "sanctified" we are "meet for the Master's use, and prepared unto every good work" (II Tim. 2:21. Alas, how many ministers even are destitute of this sanctifying grace, this baptism of the Holy Ghost! Considering this, it is not surprising that the world is filled with conflicting doctrines and beliefs. It is the function of the Holy Spirit to — teach men and "guide them into all truth." Since the dispensation of the Holy Ghost began at Pentecost, God desires that all his ministers be "filled with the Holy Ghost." His command to them is to tarry until they are "endued with power from on high." What the world needs today is a Holy Ghost ministry. However, all of the saved are "workers together with" God (II Cor. 6:1), and all need this infilling of the Holy Spirit, that they may indeed be vessels "unto honor, sanctified, and meet for the Master's use, and prepared unto every good work" (II Tim. 2:21).

People have preached and written much about the evidence of the baptism of the Holy Ghost. But to ask for our evidence that we have the Holy Spirit is like asking for an evidence of the existence of the sun overhead. The sun does not need a witness to testify for it, *it stands for itself;* and the work which it performs—illuminating the earth and kissing the face of nature with its genial rays of light and warmth, causing vegetation to spring forth, bringing life and joy, happiness and health, to the sons of men—proclaims unmistakably, without further witness, the sun and his glory. Likewise the Holy Ghost stands for himself as the witness. "The Spirit itself beareth witness with our spirit" (Rom. 8: 16; Heb. 10: 15); while the works which he performs—purifying the heart, teaching, comforting, guiding, unifying—show forth his power and glory.

The foregoing contains briefly the New Testament teaching relative to the Holy Spirit—what he is to every individual who receives him. The Holy Spirit *himself,* being bestowed by the Father upon the individual believer, is "the gift of the Holy Ghost." This is shown clearly in the case of the household of Cornelius (Acts 10: 44-45).

In addition to performing his regular office work in the heart, the Holy Spirit confers upon certain people who receive him the ability to perform special works, and these special endowments are termed "gifts of the Holy Ghost." We read of these particularly in I Corinthians 12.

In verses 1, 4-7 we find that these spiritual gifts are simply manifestations of the Spirit, and that they are *not* given to all alike, even though all be in possession of "the same Spirit." Notice the next verses: "For to one is given by the Spirit the word of wisdom; to another the word of knowledge by the same Spirit; to another faith by the same Spirit; to another the gifts of healing by the same Spirit; to another the working of miracles; to another prophecy; to another discerning of spirits; to another divers kinds of tongues; to another the interpretation of tongues; but all these worketh that one and the self-same Spirit, dividing to every man severally as he will" (vss. 8-11). (See also vss. 27-30.)

Now, if we will study the apostolic church as revealed in the New Testament, we shall be able to see all these special gifts manifested, some in one person and some in another; for all were necessary to the completeness of the church. Viewed as individuals, not every one who received the baptism of the Holy Ghost received the special gift of prophecy or the gift of working miracles or the gift of tongues. It is only by perverting the Scriptures that people can build up a claim that any one of these gifts was manifested in all who received the baptism of the Spirit.

Some False Opinions

1. *All who receive the baptism of the Holy Ghost speak in tongues as the evidence.* The verses quoted from I Corinthians 12 plainly contradict this position, for they show that the gift of tongues is no more general among those who have received the Holy Ghost than is the gift of prophecy or the gift of healing or the gift of miracles or any other of the special gifts mentioned. Nor is there any difference between the gift of tongues and speaking with tongues; these expressions *are used interchangeably* in this chapter, referring to exactly the same thing, just as the gift of prophecy and "are all prophets?" or the gift of miracles and "workers of miracles" are equivalent expressions. (Compare verses 4-11 with verses 29-31.)

The Word does not say that the gift of tongues, or speaking in tongues, is *the* evidence of the Spirit's reception; it is mentioned here simply as a "manifestation of the Spirit," in common with other special manifestations that may or may not belong to any particular individual.

The Holy Spirit must not be confounded with one of his works, so that he himself is denied unless he chooses to manifest himself in some particular manner. He himself is the satisfactory evidence. "Whereof the Holy Ghost also is a witness" (Heb. 10:15). "The Spirit itself beareth witness with our spirit" (Rom. 8:16).

In the New Testament we have records of three occasions on which people spoke with tongues when they received the baptism of the Holy Ghost: on the Day of Pentecost (Acts 2) —one hundred and twenty believers (1:15); certain disciples at Ephesus—twelve in number (19:1-7); and the household of Cornelius—number unknown (chap. 10). The total number on these three occasions was probably less than two hundred. In the Book of the Acts we have the record of many, perhaps thousands, who received the baptism of the Holy Ghost, in which no mention whatever is made concerning tongues. Some say that that part was omitted. If people desire to build up a Bible doctrine they should establish it on what the Bible says, and not on what was left out.

2. *There are three works of grace.* This teaching says that people are first converted, afterwards "receive the Holy Ghost," then still later are baptized with the Holy Ghost. This is entirely false, as will be shown by many Bible texts. The only apparent proof of that position seems to be John 20:22, where it is recorded that Christ, after his resurrection, appeared to his disciples and "breathed on them, and saith unto them, Receive ye the Holy Ghost." This occurred several days before they were baptized with the Holy Ghost on Pentecost.

But a particular examination of the circumstances connected with John 20:22 shows that the disciples did not *at that time* receive the Holy Ghost, but that the verse is an allusion to Pentecost; for this was the same occasion described in Luke 24:33 ff., where the reference to the Spirit is given in other language, as follows: "But tarry ye in the city of Jerusalem, until ye be endued with power from on high" (vs. 49). We know that this refers to Pentecost. (Compare Acts 1:8.)

The crowning proof that there is no difference between receiving the Holy Ghost and being baptized with the Holy Ghost is the fact that in the labors of the Apostles themselves the two are identified as one and the same thing. Paul asked the disciples at Ephesus, "Have ye received the Holy Ghost since ye believed?" (Acts 19:2), and they replied that they had not even heard of the Holy Ghost; therefore, they did not have him in this sense. "And when Paul had laid his hands upon them, the Holy Ghost came on them; and they spake with tongues, and prophesied" (vs. 6). Now, this baptism of the Holy Ghost, accompanied by tongues and prophecy, was identical with receiving the Holy Ghost. Thus these disciples experienced only two works of grace.

When Peter and John came down and prayed for the disciples at Samaria "that they might receive the Holy Ghost: (for as yet he was fallen upon none of them). . . . Then laid they their hands upon them, and they received the Holy Ghost. And when Simon saw that through laying on of the apostles' hands the Holy Ghost was given, he offered them money, saying, Give me also this power, that on whomsoever I lay hands, he may receive the Holy Ghost. But Peter said unto him, Thy money perish with thee, because thou hast thought that the gift of God may be purchased with money" (Acts 8:15-20). There is no possible way of evading the fact that in this case the "gift of God," the "gift of the Holy Ghost," "receiving the Holy Ghost," and the Holy Ghost "falling" upon disciples are all one and the same thing—a second work in believers.

So also with the household of Cornelius, as recorded in Acts 10:44-47; 11:15-17; 15:8-9.

Temptations

I would not have the reader think that the sanctified life places the individual beyond the reach of temptation. Entire sanctification does not deprive us of that which is essentially human, but we are purged from sinful, carnal elements received through the Fall, and our human natures are brought into line with the divine, so that our desires are wholly to please God. But we are capable of temptation along natural lines. Christ himself "was in all points tempted like as we are," but he overcame every temptation as our example, and we should take courage and move forward. One of Christ's special temptations had a perfectly legitimate basis in the natural desire for food (Matt. 4:1-4); and another involved that which was not right—great possessions for the purpose of worldly honor (vs. 8).

God has a definite purpose in allowing us to be tempted. It is for our good. Be encouraged, for "there hath no temptation taken you but such as is common to man: but God is faithful, who will not suffer you to be tempted above that ye are able; but will with the temptation also make a way to escape, that ye may be able to bear it" (I Cor. 10:13).

Now, we cannot be tempted and tried without feeling tempted and tried. Peter says that "for a season, if need be, ye are in heaviness through manifold temptations" (I Pet. 1:6). There is no mistake about this matter: the sanctified person who is being deeply tempted or tried does not feel just the same as at other times. On certain occasions Christ himself felt "grieved," and his soul was stirred within him; but the records of these occurrences fail to show any carnal stirring or actions proceeding from an impure heart. So, reader, it must be with you. In seasons of trial and trouble, remember that the Lord "giveth more grace. Wherefore he saith, God resisteth the proud, but giveth grace unto the humble. Submit yourselves therefore to God. Resist the devil, and he will flee from you" (Jas. 4:6-7).

The Spirit-Filled Life

This experience of entire sanctification is indeed a blessed one. While the justified life must be kept free from outward acts of sin, the wholly sanctified life is the complete harmony of the individual, both internally and externally, with the perfect will of God. All evil affections, our spiritual enemies, are gone; the soul is pure. The Lord grants unto us "that we being delivered out of the hand of our enemies might serve him without fear, in holiness and righteousness before him, all the days of our life" (Luke 1:74-75). Yea, it is his will that "we should live soberly, righteously, and godly, in this present world; looking for that blessed hope, and the glorious appearing of the great God and our Savior Jesus Christ; who gave himself for us, that he might redeem us from all iniquity, and purify unto himself a peculiar people, zealous of good works" (Titus 2:12-14).

In this happy condition we are able to "bring forth more fruit"; therefore the fruit of the Spirit is developed in us abundantly. The first thing mentioned in Paul's catalogue of the fruits of the Spirit is love. Love is felt by the justified soul, but when we enter the second, or standing, grace (Rom. 5:1-2) "the love of God is shed abroad in our hearts by the Holy Ghost which is given unto us" (vs. 5).

What a blessing is this life of entire sanctification! What a power in the hands of God is a Spirit-filled church! Someone, commenting on the baptism of the Holy Ghost, said: " 'When he is come . . . unto you' . . . you will become a storm center of a new and mighty evangelism, and all the forces of evil cannot keep back the incoming tides of saving grace." "Blessed are the pure in heart: for they shall see God" (Matt. 5:8).

Chapter 10

DIVINE HEALING

Divine Healing in Prophecy

The prophets of old predicted a special manifestation of healing power when Christ should appear. Isaiah, speaking of the coming of God's "Servant," for whose law men should wait, said that he was to be "a light of the Gentiles" and that he should "open the blind eyes . . . bring out the prisoners from the prison, and them that sit in darkness out of the prison house" (42:6-7).

Christ claimed the fulfillment of these prophecies in himself. While preaching in the synagogue at Nazareth, he read aloud Isaiah 61:1-2 and applied it to himself.

Again Isaiah makes mention of these things: "Say to them that are of a fearful heart, Be strong, fear not: behold, your God will come with vengeance, even God with a recompense; he will come and save you. Then the eyes of the blind shall be opened, and the ears of the deaf shall be unstopped. Then shall the lame man leap as an hart, and the tongue of the dumb sing" (35:4-6).

This prediction of healing manifestation by Christ was perfectly fulfilled, as we read in Matthew 8:16-17 and 11:4-5.

This healing work was also predicted by Malachi, who said, "But unto you that fear my name shall the Sun of righteousness arise with healing in his wings; and ye shall go forth, and grow up as calves of the stall" (4:2).

Manifested by Christ

The Scriptures show that Christ manifested himself marvelously as a healer. This work of physical ministration went hand in hand with the message of salvation. "And Jesus went about all Galilee, teaching in their synagogues, and preaching the gospel of the kingdom, and healing all manner of sickness and all manner of disease among the people. And his fame went throughout all Syria: and they brought unto him all sick people that were taken with divers diseases and torments, and those which were possessed with devils, and those which were lunatic, and those that had the palsy; and he healed them" (Matt. 4:23-24). (See also 9:2-6; 15:30-31.)

The Gospels abound with such instances. It is asserted by many that Jesus performed these works of healing for the purpose of establishing his claim as the Messiah. There is no doubt that this was one purpose, and a most important one; for Peter says that Jesus of Nazareth was "approved of God among you by miracles and wonders and signs" (Acts 2:22). Such manifestations of superhuman power were necessary in order to convince men that Jesus was no ordinary man.

The record shows, however, that another motive also figured in the case—Jesus' compassion. "Jesus went about all the cities and villages, teaching in their synagogues, and preaching the gospel of the kingdom, and healing every sickness and every disease among the people. But when he saw the multitudes, he was moved with compassion on them" (Matt. 9:35-36). "And Jesus went forth, and saw a great multitude, and was moved with compassion toward them, and he healed their sick" (14:14).

Manifested by the Apostles

The same mighty power accompanied the preaching of the Apostles. "And when he had called unto him his twelve disciples, he gave them power against unclean spirits, to cast them out, and to heal all manner of sickness and all manner of diseases" (Matt. 10:1). He then sent them out, saying, "As ye go, preach, saying, The kingdom of heaven is at hand. Heal the sick, cleanse the lepers, raise the dead, cast out devils: freely ye have received, freely give" (vss. 7-8). "And they went out, and preached that men should repent. And they cast out many devils, and anointed with oil many that were sick, and healed them" (Mark 6:12-13).

Permanent in the Church

It is asserted by some today that divine healing ceased with the Apostles; but it is a historical fact, easily verified, that it was perpetuated in the early church. Of course, these divine works will quickly cease with unbelievers, but they "shall follow them that believe." That they were intended to be permanent in the church is clearly shown by the Scriptures. The commission of world-wide evangelism given to the Apostles, in which these works were promised, was to continue "even unto the end of the world" (Matt. 28:19-20 with Mark 16:15-18). Therefore, in I Corinthians 12 we find all the special gifts of the Spirit placed in the normal church, the Spirit "dividing to every man severally as he will." "And God hath set some in the church, first apostles, secondarily prophets, thirdly teachers, after that miracles, then gifts of healing, helps, governments, diversities of tongues" (vs. 28). If God has placed these functions in his church, who dares to deny the fact or to attempt to take them out?

When Christ sent his disciples forth to preach "he gave them power against unclean spirits, to cast them out, and to heal all manner of sickness and all manner of disease" (Matt. 10:1). The Apostles realized that they had this power; therefore when Peter and John met the lame man at the gate Beautiful, Peter could say to him boldly, "Silver and gold have I none; but such as I have give I thee: In the name of Jesus Christ of Nazareth rise up and walk" (Acts 3:6).

But this is not all. The ministry of healing belongs to all God's ministers and is a part of their regular work. Knowing this, James could without hesitation instruct suffering men and women what to do in case of sickness. Here are his words: "Is any sick among you? let him call for the elders of the church; and let them pray over him, anointing him with oil in the name of the Lord: and the prayer of faith shall save the sick, and the Lord shall raise him up; and if he have committed sins, they shall be forgiven him. Confess your faults one to another, and pray one for another, that ye may be healed. The effectual fervent prayer of a righteous man availeth much" (Jas. 5:14-16).

Divine healing as taught in the Bible is not mind healing or Christian Science (?) healing. It is healing wrought by the direct power of God. Most of the cures performed by these counterfeit healing systems are easily accounted for on psychological grounds, as being *subjective*—the natural result of the power of mind over matter. Therefore they may succeed to a certain extent, particularly in treating functional disorders. But this principle is not new. Physicians in all ages have known how important it is to secure the favorable action of the mind of the patient, encouraging him in the belief that he will be restored to health; for when the patient despairs of life, it is difficult to do anything for him along natural lines.

But divine healing is *objective*—*it is from without*. It is the power of God bestowed directly upon the individual. Organic diseases yield to the mighty power of our Christ as readily as mere functional disorders. "Jesus Christ the same yesterday, and today, and forever" (Heb. 13:8). He has lost none of his power, he has not forsaken his people, and he is therefore able and ready to fulfill his promises.

Is it certain that it is his will to heal? First of all, let me say that the will of God is revealed in his Word. "And, behold, there came a leper and worshiped him, saying, Lord, if thou wilt, thou canst make me clean" (Matt. 8:2). This man was sure of Christ's ability to do the work, but was not certain of his will in the matter. "And Jesus put forth his hand, and touched him, saying, I will; be thou clean. And immediately his leprosy was cleansed" (vs. 3).

Yes, dear reader, it is his will to heal. "We have not an high priest which cannot be touched with the feeling of our infirmities. . . . Let us therefore come boldly unto the throne of grace, that we may obtain mercy, and find grace to help in time of need" (Heb. 4:15-16). It can still be said of him, "He was moved with compassion toward them, and he healed their sick" (Matt. 14:14).

The subject of divine healing appears to be somewhat complicated, however, by the revelation of two aspects of God's will. Thus, he has revealed his willingness to heal, saying that "the prayer of faith shall save the sick, and the Lord shall raise him up" (Jas. 5:15), but he has also declared that "it is appointed unto men once to die" (Heb. 9:27), showing thereby that a time will come in every life when the person will not be "raised up." This, of course, does not mean that in the last earthly hours the individual cannot receive physical help in the way of alleviation of pain and suffering, but he will not be "raised up."

The question for the person who believes in divine healing, then, is: "Is it God's will at this time to heal me?" Can we find out God's will in this matter? Yes. "Be not unwise, but understanding what the will of the Lord is" (Eph. 5:17). It is by the "prayer of faith" that the person is raised up to health again; and faith for healing requires the special inspiration of the Holy Spirit. In fact, in many cases "we know not what we should pray for as we ought: but the Spirit itself maketh intercession for us with groanings which cannot be uttered" (Rom. 8:26). We may be sure that the real "prayer of faith" for perfect healing and restoration cannot be offered when it is to the glory of God to take the person home to himself. But in other cases (which the Spirit of God will make clear to those who are spiritual, believing, and obedient) it is God's will to heal; and we should "come boldly to the throne of grace" for this blessing.

Conditions for Healing

The plan of healing set forth in the New Testament is not arbitrary, but conditional. We must understand and conform to the standard of the Word if we hope to receive its benefits. Faith is always required of the individual who is seeking healing when he is capable of exercising it, or of someone else. For confirmation of this statement consult Matthew 8:13; 9:2, 29; Mark 5:34, 36; 9:23; John 4:50.

Sources of Disease

But there are other conditions of a more particular nature, and these are dependent upon the reasons for the disease and the source from which it came. The Scriptures plainly teach that sickness and disease are now brought upon us by causes proceeding from three different sources: (1) nature, (2) Satan, (3) God himself. These we shall consider separately.

A large part of men's afflictions are directly traceable to natural causes. "His bones are full of the sin of his youth, which shall lie down with him in the dust" (Job 20:11). Overwork and mental strain, as in the cases of Daniel and Epaphroditus:

"And I Daniel fainted, and was sick certain days" (Dan. 8:27);
"He [Epaphroditus] was sick nigh unto death: but God had
mercy on him. . . . Because for the work of Christ he was nigh
unto death, not regarding his life, to supply your lack of
service toward me" (Phil. 2:27, 30). "In the day of our king
the princes have made him sick with bottles of wine" (Hos.
7:5).

Satan afflicts. "And ought not this woman, being a daughter
of Abraham, whom Satan hath bound, lo, these eighteen years,
be loosed from this bond?" (Luke 13:16). "How God anointed
Jesus of Nazareth with the Holy Ghost and with power: who
went about doing good, and healing all that were oppressed of
the devil; for God was with him" (Acts 10:38). "So went Satan
forth from the presence of the Lord, and smote Job with sore
boils from the sole of his foot unto his crown" (Job 2:7).

The afflictions which God administers are not always per-
missive, as in the case of Job, but are frequently direct. God
is not the author of moral evil, but he is the direct author, in
many cases, of physical evil, either in the entire destruction
of wrongdoers, as in the threatened overthrow of the Nine-
vites (Jonah 3:10), or in the destruction or affliction of individuals as a direct punishment for sin. God has always dealt
with men thus. "Behold therefore the goodness and severity of
God: on them which fell, severity" (Rom. 11:22).

The cases of this kind are numerous, "O full of all subtilty
and all mischief, thou child of the devil, thou enemy of all
righteousness, wilt thou not cease to pervert the right ways
of the Lord? And now, behold, the hand of the Lord is upon
thee, and thou shalt be blind, not seeing the sun for a season.
And immediately there fell on him a mist and a darkness; and
he went about seeking some to lead him by the hand" (Acts
13:10-11). "Because of the wickedness of thy doings, whereby
thou hast forsaken me. The Lord shall make the pestilence
cleave unto thee" (Deut. 28:20-21). (See also Lev. 26:14-16;
II Sam. 12:15.)

In view of these three causes of sickness and disease, how
precious are these words of the psalmist! "Bless the Lord, O
my soul; and all that is within me, bless his holy name. Bless
the Lord, O my soul, and forget not all his benefits: who for-

giveth all thine iniquities; who healeth all thy diseases" (Ps. 103:1-3).

It is evident that God is the only one who can heal all diseases. If an affliction or sickness originates in natural causes, it may possibly be cured by natural means. Such diseases constitute the special province wherein earthly physicians are able to operate. If a disease is a direct imposition of Satan, he may remove his hand of affliction, thus effecting a cure of the individual. It is also possible that Satan may have the power to remove afflictions originating in natural causes. But when God himself punishes men by affliction, because of their sins, he alone can reach such a case and effect a cure.

This makes clear the special conditions that the applicant must meet in order to obtain divine healing. If by intemperance or carelessness we are ourselves responsible for our afflictions, then when we call for the elders of the church we are instructed, "Confess your faults one to another, and pray one for another, that ye may be healed" (Jas. 5:16). If we are living to please God, and Satan imposes sickness upon us we can rebuke the devil in the name of the Lord, and God will grant healing. But when God has himself laid the hand of affliction upon us because of our own sins, then conditions are entirely different. Neither man nor Satan can effect the cure. The conditions for divine healing in such cases are well set forth in the circumstance concerning Miriam. Before healing can be obtained, sin must be confessed. "And Aaron said unto Moses, Alas, my lord, I beseech thee, lay not the sin upon us, wherein we have done foolishly, and wherein we have sinned. . . . And Moses cried unto the Lord, saying, Heal her now, O God, I beseech thee" (Num. 12:11-13). The instruction given in James covers this point: "If he have committed sins, they shall be forgiven him" (5:15).

I cannot close this chapter without saying that at the present time these signs are following "them that believe." The primitive gospel of salvation and healing is now being proclaimed by a Holy Ghost ministry with the results set forth in the Scriptures. Personally, I have witnessed the healing of many thousands of people, of nearly all diseases, including deafness, total blindness, heart trouble, pneumonia, tuberculosis, and others. From childhood I have known this truth, and I have frequently been healed myself.

"Oh that men would praise the Lord for his goodness, and for his wonderful works to the children of men"; for he is the one "who forgiveth all thine iniquities; who healeth all thy diseases."

CONCERNING THE CHURCH

Chapter 11

THE UNITY OF BELIEVERS

As we have already shown, the definite and instantaneous experience that makes us living members of Christ is the new birth; and as we thus become members of the family of God, we also by the same act and experience become members of all those who are members of the divine family. "We are members one of another" (Eph. 4:25). "One is your Master, even Christ; and all ye are brethren" (Matt. 23:8). "Behold, how good and how pleasant it is for brethren to dwell together in unity!" (Ps. 133:1). "Endeavoring to keep the unity of the Spirit in the bond of peace" (Eph. 4:3).

So complete and perfect is this Bible standard of divine relationship, of spiritual unity among all the saved, that they are declared to constitute one body in Christ. We are reconciled "unto God in one body by the cross" (Eph. 2:16). "Ye are called in one body" (Col. 3:15). (Also see I Cor. 12:13; Eph. 5:30.) This represents the closest possible union, both with Christ and with one another.

Unity Illustrated

In different passages the Apostle Paul uses the natural body to illustrate the spiritual body, composed of all the truly saved. "For as we have many members in one body, and all members have not the same office: so we, being many, are one body in Christ, and every one members one of another" (Rom. 12: 4-5).

There is perfect harmony in a normal body, for its unity is not effected by external means, but is *organic*. Many and diverse though the members be, still they are all necessary for the completeness and harmony of the whole. So it is with the body of Christ. We are many members, differing in age, in sex, in intellectual attainments, in material possessions, in social advantages, in nationality; still, it can truthfully be said, "There is neither Jew nor Greek, there is neither bond nor free, there is neither male nor female: for ye are all one in Christ Jesus" (Gal. 3:28).

The body of Christ is "subject unto Christ," its head (Eph. 5:24), therefore we all have "one mind" (II Cor. 13:11), "the mind of Christ" (I Cor. 2:16), and are able "to be likeminded one toward another" and "with one mind and one mouth glorify God, even the Father of our Lord Jesus Christ" (Rom. 15:5-6).

In One Body

One purpose of Christ's death was that "he should gather together in one the children of God that were scattered abroad" (John 11:52). Jesus himself said, "Other sheep I have [Gentiles], which are not of this [Jewish] fold: them also I must bring, and they shall hear my voice; and there shall be one fold [flock], and one shepherd" (10:16).

In the second chapter of Ephesians we read how these two classes of people were made one. Although "in time past" the Gentiles were "strangers from the covenants of promise, having no hope, and without God in the world . . . [they were] made nigh by the blood of Christ. For he is our peace, who hath made both [Jews and Gentiles] one, and hath broken down the middle wall of partition between us . . . that he might reconcile both unto God in one body by the cross, having slain the enmity thereby" (Eph. 2:12-16). This unification of peoples so diverse was not effected by Jews becoming Gentiles or by the Gentiles becoming Jews, but by both accepting Christ as "the way, the truth and the life" and rejecting all that was antagonistic to Christ and his truth.

The prayer of Christ recorded in John 17 shows the sacredness of this doctrine of unity. He prayed, "Sanctify them through thy truth: thy word is truth. . . . That they all may be one; as thou, Father, art in me, and I in thee, that they also may be one in us: that the world may believe that thou hast sent me. . . . I in them, and thou in me, that they may be made perfect in one" (vss. 17, 21, 23).

Though salvation itself brings us into a divine relationship with each other, the indwelling evil nature prevents the full realization of that perfect unity of heart which Christ so much desired, and for which he most earnestly prayed. The Apostle Paul, writing to the church at Corinth, mentions the strife and division over preachers that was manifested among certain brethren there and attributes it to the fact that they were "yet carnal" (I Cor. 3:1-5). But sanctification purifies the heart, destroying carnality, and therefore makes the people of God "perfect in one." (See Acts 4:31-33.)

Even the idea of division among Christians was foreign to the pure apostolic church (Rom. 16:17). To the Corinthians Paul said, "I beseech you, brethren, . . . that ye all speak the same thing, and that there be no divisions among you; but that ye be perfectly joined together in the same mind and in the same judgment" (I Cor. 1:10).

Unity Through Relationship

The underlying foundation of true Christian unity is *relationship*, not development or attainments.

We are "all one in Christ Jesus." What does it mean to be *in Christ*? First of all, it means to be "born again," for without this experience we are not Christians at all and "cannot see the kingdom of God" (John 3:3). "There is therefore now no condemnation to them which are in Christ Jesus" (Rom. 8:1). Why? Because they have been "made free from the law of sin and death" (vs. 2). To be in Christ, then, signifies to be born of God and to have our sins removed by his grace (II Cor. 5:17; I John 3:6). By this spiritual birth we enter the spiritual family, where we possess the divine life which flows in all its members, and are thus "all one in Christ Jesus" by virtue of a spiritual blood relationship.

Unity Perfected

But we must also develop in spiritual life, attainments, and behavior in such a practical, visible manner "that the world may believe." We must "dwell together in unity"; we must "all speak the same thing." Now, how is this possible? How can those who are one in spirit, by virtue of spiritual birth, be made "perfect in one" before the world, so as to convince unbelievers of the truth of Christianity? The conditions for this perfect unity are expressly stated in John 17, where Christ's prayer for the unity of his people is recorded:

1. *We must be "in Christ,"* which signifies salvation from sin—"not of the world" (vs. 16).

2. *We must receive the Word of God and keep it,* which requires the rejection of all contrary doctrines and commandments of men.

3. *We must be kept in the Father's name only.* "Holy Father, keep through thine own name those whom thou hast given me, that they may be one, as we are" (vs. 11).

4. *We must be sanctified wholly,* which removes from the heart the cause of carnal divisions.

There is a standard of so-called unity made prominent throughout Christendom, which is simply an attempt to bring together by external organization the professed followers of Christ. This may be in the form of human denominational organization, or in the grouping together of a number of such individual organizations, but such can never be more than a counterfeit. True unity is of the heart and can be effected only by meeting Bible conditions. Mere external organization— bringing together multitudes of people, the majority of whom know nothing about a saved experience and sinless life and never have been born again—is not in any sense an exhibition of true Bible unity. Bible unity is based on spiritual life and is in accordance with the Word and Spirit of God. The truly saved have spiritual fellowship with each other, and know each other, and have no spiritual affinity with those who are not of God. They "have no fellowship with the unfruitful works of darkness, but rather reprove them" (Eph. 5:11). They are instructed to "stand fast in one spirit" (Phil. 1:27).

Not one text in the New Testament teaches that division among God's people is right, but everywhere unity is enjoined and division denounced. We read of one Lord, one salvation, one God, one faith, one Spirit, one mind, one mouth, one body, one baptism, one new and living way, one Savior, and one heaven. And in order to serve this one God aright, follow this one Lord according to his one new and living way, and obey his one revealed Word, we must be "all one in Christ Jesus."

Chapter 12

THE NEW TESTAMENT CHURCH

Matthew 16:18 introduces into the gospel history the subject of the church. There Jesus says, "I will build my church; and the gates of hell shall not prevail against it." This text implies that the church as an institution was not yet founded and that Christ himself was to be the founder and builder of his church.

Before proceeding to set forth the New Testament church, however, let us first notice

The Church in Type

The church of God is often referred to as the house of God, his spiritual dwelling place on earth. In Old Testament times the house of God was an earthly structure: first the tabernacle, constructed in the wilderness (Exod. 25:8); afterwards, the temple at Jerusalem (II Chron. 5:1). At the dedication of the first house, or tabernacle, God manifested himself in it in such a glorious manner that "Moses was not able to enter into the tent of the congregation, because . . . the glory of the Lord filled the tabernacle" (Exod. 40:35). So also at the dedication of Solomon's temple (I Kings 8:11).

Now, though such earthly structures constituted the house of God in that dispensation, the prophets clearly predicted that when the Messiah came he would build another house of God. (See Zech. 6:12-13.) In fulfillment of these prophecies Christ says, "I will build my church."

The writer of the Book of Hebrews affirms that the Old Testament house of God was "a figure for the time then present," pointing forward to, and meeting its antitype in, "a greater and more perfect tabernacle," which was introduced by Christ and dedicated with his own blood (Heb. 9:1-14). That the church is now the house of God is further shown in I Timothy 3:15; I Peter 2:5; and Ephesians 2:21-22.

Now let us notice some Bible characteristics of this church.

89

The Body of Christ

We should divest our minds of current ideas of formal church organization and earnestly seek to understand the real significance of that church of which Christ personally was the founder. A few texts make this point clear: "And hath put all things under his [Christ's] feet, and gave him to be the head over all things to the church, which is his body, the fullness of him that filleth all in all" (Eph. 1:22-23). The church, then, is the body of Christ. Of this body Jesus himself is the head (Col. 1:18, 24). In these texts "body" and "church" are used interchangeably, referring to one and the same thing. The body of which Christ is the head is the church that he built, "the church of God, which he hath purchased with his own blood" (Acts 20:28).

It is therefore to Calvary that we must look for the specific act by which Christ personally became the founder of his church. *There* it was "purchased with his own blood." *There* we find the application of those sublime words of the Savior: "And I, if I be lifted up from the earth, will draw all men unto me" (John 12:32). By virtue of that act God "put all things under his [Christ's] feet, and gave him to be the head over all things to the church." By virtue of that act "God also hath highly exalted him, and given him a name which is above every name" (Phil. 2:9). The church, then, proceeds from Calvary. Pentecost was but its initial manifestation to men and its dedication for service.

The Mode of Membership

Since by his death Christ purposed to draw all men unto him, it is evident that all members of Christ are therefore members of his body, the church. To this agree the words of the Apostle Paul: "Now hath God set the members every one of them in the body, as it hath pleased him" (I Cor. 12:18). (Also Rom. 12:4-5.)

Becoming a member in the spiritual body of Christ is necessarily a spiritual operation. Men may admit members to a formal relationship in a humanly organized group called a church, but the Spirit of God alone can make us members of

Christ. "For by one Spirit are we all baptized [or inducted] into one body, whether we be Jews or Gentiles, whether we be bond or free; and have been all made to drink into one Spirit" (I Cor. 12:13). This text does not refer to literal water baptism, but to the work of the Spirit by which we are inducted into Christ. "God hath set the members every one of them in the body" (vs. 18). And since this is the work of the Spirit, it is evident that none but the saved can possibly find admittance into the spiritual body of Christ. Under a different figure Jesus conveys the same truth: "I am the door: by me if any man enter in, he shall be saved" (John 10:9). "And the Lord added to them [the church] day by day those that were saved" (Acts 2:47, ASV). Salvation, then, is the condition of membership.

The members of Christ are members of God's family. How do we become members of the divine family? "Except a man be born again, he cannot see the kingdom of God" (John 3:3). (See also John 1:12-13; I John 3:2.) Since this family, or church, is composed of the saved, or those who are born again, and excludes all the unsaved, we can understand Paul's reference to "a glorious church, not having spot, or wrinkle, or any such thing; but . . . holy and without blemish" (Eph. 5:27).

The Visibility of the Church

In the apostolic church God's power in redemption brought into the lives of believers forces that could not but unite them in a social unit. It drew them together in living sympathy and united their hearts firmly in the strong bonds of brotherly love. Their outward organic union as a church was the natural and inevitable result of this inward life and love.

The local church was not merely an aggregate of individuals accidentally gathered together, but was the local, concrete embodiment of the spiritual body of Christ, the unified company of regenerated persons who as a body were dedicated to Christ, acknowledged of Christ, and used by Christ through the Holy Spirit for the accomplishment of his work. Jerusalem furnishes the first example, dating from Pentecost (Acts 2).

Membership in the general body of Christ was conditioned solely on the new birth, or salvation. Since the individual congregation was the local embodiment of the general church, none but the saved could properly become members thereof. But the bringing together of many individuals in one assembly involved also a social element and required the principle of *recognition*. There is no evidence, however, that such recognition was given by a formal, official act of the church in its corporate capacity. Since salvation is of the heart, it was possible for human recognition to miss its true purpose temporarily, as when the unworthy Ananias and Sapphira were recognized in the local church at Jerusalem and, at another time, the converted Saul was temporarily barred from fellowship (Acts 9:26).

The local church at Jerusalem did not cease to be the church of God because two unworthy persons obtained temporary recognition in it. This incident gave occasion for the church to manifest its inherent life by its ability to discern and then cast off the offenders, just as an earthly physical body casts off effete matter. As a result of the judgment pronounced on Ananias and Sapphira, "great fear came upon all the church. . . . And of the rest durst no man join himself to them: but the people magnified them" (Acts 5:11, 13). The fiery judgments of God put an end to that imposition, with the result that "believers were the more added to the Lord, multitudes both of men and women" (vs. 14). "And the Lord added to them day by day those that were saved" (2:47, ASV).

The physical body may experience the mutilation of some of its members and still survive, but there is a limit beyond which death will ensue. Likewise the spiritual body, the local congregation, may survive the encumbrance of a few false members who have by some means succeeded in gaining temporary recognition as Christians; but from the general facts and principles already adduced we may safely assert that a local church is a church of God only so long as it is able to function properly *as a body*. As long as the Spirit of God is in the ascendancy so that the people of God as a body manifest the power of God, maintain the truth of God, are filled with the Spirit of God, and are actually used by the Spirit in performing the works of God, so long are they the church of God. Whenever another spirit gains the ascendancy and the divine, spiritual characteristics are lost to view, then is fulfilled that which is written: "I will spue thee out of my mouth." Henceforth their condition is like that of Sardis, "Thou hast a name that thou livest, and art dead" (Rev. 3:1). Such dead congregations are no longer a part of the true church and are unworthy of the recognition of spiritual congregations.

The Name of the Church

According to the New Testament the followers of Jesus, as individuals, are called friends, disciples, brethren, saints. As a church the disciples took the name of their Father, as Jesus prayed that they would, in order to manifest their unity in him (see John 17:11); therefore we read: "Unto the church of God" (I Cor. 1:2; II Cor. 1:1); "I persecuted the church of God" (Gal. 1:13); "Despise ye the church of God?" (I Cor. 11:22); "Give no offense . . . to the church of God" (10:32); "Take care of the church of God" (I Tim. 3:5); "Feed the church of God, which he hath purchased with his own blood" (Acts 20:28).

The Discipline of the Church

The discipline of the church was simply "the law of Christ," first as delivered orally by Christ personally, then by specially inspired apostles, and afterwards expressed by them in written form in the Christian Scriptures. "I have given them thy word" (John 17:14). "All scripture is given by inspiration of God, and is profitable for doctrine, for reproof, for correction, for instruction in righteousness: that the man of God may be perfect, throughly furnished unto all good works" (II Tim. 3:16-17).

Doctrine, reproof, correction, and instruction cover all the essential ground of discipline; therefore the Bible is the only necessary rule of faith and practice. In fact, the disciplines of many of the Protestant churches state that the Bible is to be accepted as the supreme Word of God and that whatever is not contained therein or cannot be proved thereby is not to be required of any man. Then why not discard all the disciplines of man, which contain a multitude of unscriptural doctrines, rules, and regulations, and just accept the Bible as the all-sufficient rule of faith?

Organization and Government

Jesus was not only the initial founder of the church but is its permanent head and governor. Isaiah, predicting the coming of Christ, declared that "the government shall be upon his shoulder" (Isa. 9:6). And again, we read that "he is the head of the body, the church . . . that in all things he might have the pre-eminence" (Col. 1:18).

The general nature of church government was, therefore, a *theocracy*. Christ was king and lawgiver, governor and administrator. His rule was a moral and spiritual dominion. It was only when the living, vital union of Christ with his church was lost to view that men began endeavoring to strengthen the bonds of external union by unscriptural human organization and human authority. In the primitive church both organization and governmental authority proceeded from Christ through the operation of the Holy Spirit. "God set the members every one of them in the body, as it pleased him" (I Cor. 12:18). He endowed them with various gifts, and these gifts, combined with all other qualifications, gave each member his particular place in the body and also determined the nature and extent of his work and authority in the body. Thus, the organization was divine. (See Eph. 4:8, 11-12; I Cor. 12; Rom. 12:4-7.)

Governmental positions in the primitive church, with their authority and responsibility, were the product of those gifts and qualifications bestowed upon certain individuals in particular. Hence, ministerial appointment was divine. God by his Spirit called his ministers directly and individually—"The Holy Ghost hath made you overseers" (Acts 20:28). The only other essential to its practical operation was recognition, and such recognition belonged, in the last analysis, to the whole church, but was formally given by the laying on of the hands of other ministers.

As we have seen, the general church in its visible phase was made up of various local congregations "set in order" by apostolic authority. So far as their own local affairs were concerned, these congregations were autonomous, but even though they were distributed over a wide territory they were not in all respects independent, isolated units. As members of Christ, sharing in a common life and engaged in a common cause, the believers were bound together in one brotherhood, by ties of fellowship and love.

Let us notice some particular points concerning the relation of members in the primitive church.

Equality in the Church

Men have always been prone to divide the race into clans, classes, and castes. But the Word of God recognizes the essential unity of the human race; it teaches that all are in one sense on the same plane because of universal sin and that all stand in need of redemption; therefore, it lifts up a standard of spiritual equality for all those who are redeemed. "Let the brother of low degree rejoice in that he is exalted: but the rich, in that he is made low" (Jas. 1:9-10). This places all on the same plane in Christ. "For by one Spirit are we all baptized into one body, whether we be Jews or Gentiles, whether we be bond or free" (I Cor. 12:13). (See also Gal. 3:28; Jas. 2:1-4.)

To the first ministers Christ said, "Be not ye called Rabbi: for one is your Master, even Christ; and all ye are brethren" (Matt. 23:8). When some of their number sought for a position of pre-eminence over the rest, Christ referred to conditions among the Gentiles, whose great men domineered over the others, and said, "It shall not be so among you; but whosoever will be great among you, let him be your minister; and whosoever will be chief among you, let him be your servant: even as the Son of man came not to be ministered unto, but to minister" (20:26-28).

While the greater gifts and qualifications of some of the Apostles made them more useful than others and placed greater responsibilities upon them, still this humble standard of equality was maintained until the Apostasy began to develop.

Christianity is the only religion in the world that recognizes men and women as equals. In paganism women are regarded as greatly inferior to men and usually have little or no place in religion, unless, indeed, it is some dishonorable connection, as in their licentious orgies. Among the Jews, even the laws of Moses made special provision for women, and they were honored and respected; some of them even rose to positions of prominence, as Deborah, who held an official position in Israel (Judg. 4:4). Christ delivered one of his greatest sermons to a woman by a well in Samaria (John 4), and a woman was the first messenger sent to proclaim the great fact of the resurrection. The Apostle Paul distinctly recognizes the equality of women with men: "There is neither Jew nor Greek, there is neither bond nor free, there is neither male nor female: for ye are all one in Christ Jesus" (Gal. 3:28).

This equality of women with men in the apostolic church extended, in some instances, even to official positions.

1. *As deaconesses.* The original Greek of Romans 16:1 clearly shows that Phoebe, a woman, was a deaconess of the church at Cenchrea. Now, "the office of a deacon" was a distinct, public, official position in the church, and its candidates were publicly ordained by the laying on of the hands of the Apostles (I Tim. 3:8-13 with Acts 6:1-6).

2. *As ministers.* Nor was the ministry of women limited to temporal affairs. We read in different texts of Priscilla and her husband, Aquila (the name of the woman sometimes standing first), and find that on one occasion they jointly took Apollos, a powerful minister of the gospel, and "expounded unto him the way of God more perfectly" (Acts 18:26). The first sermon concerning the Christ was preached in the temple to the people of Jerusalem by Anna the prophetess—a woman (Luke 2:36-38). The Samaritan woman whom Jesus met at the well went into her city and proclaimed Christ to the people, with the result that "many of the Samaritans of that city believed on him for the saying of the woman" (John 4:39). On the Day of Pentecost the Spirit of God was poured out publicly upon the women, and they prophesied in the presence of the wondering multitudes. Philip the evangelist "had four daughters, virgins, which did prophesy" (Acts 21:8-9).

Now, what does it mean to prophesy? The primary signification of the term is *to speak forth,* to tell out the message or the mysteries of God. Its secondary meaning (in some respects the outgrowth of the first) is *to foretell future events.* Paul clearly shows that through the "gift of prophecy" we may "understand all mysteries, and all knowledge" (II Cor. 13:2).

To prophesy, then, is to proclaim the mysteries and knowledge of God. (See also I Cor. 2:7-14.)

To preach the gospel of Christ, then, under the inspiration of the Holy Ghost is to proclaim the "mysteries," the "hidden wisdom" of God—*to prophesy.* This is the application which the Apostle himself makes of the term (I Cor. 14:3).

Peter declares that the Pentecostal experience, when the women spoke "as the Spirit gave them utterance," was a fulfillment of the prophet Joel's prediction that "on my servants and on my handmaidens I will pour out in those days of my Spirit; and they shall prophesy" (Acts 2:4, 14-18, with 1:14-15). The Jerusalem church was composed of "multitudes both of men and women" (5:14), and when persecution arose "they were all scattered abroad . . . except the apostles. . . . Therefore they that were scattered abroad went everywhere preaching the word" (8:1, 4). If they were all scattered and they all went preaching, much of that preaching was by women.

From many considerations it is evident that Paul recognized women's place in the gospel. He wrote to the Philippians, "Help those women which labored with me in the gospel, with Clement also, and with other my fellow laborers, whose names are in the book of life" (4:3). Clement was a minister, and these women are ranked with him and others as Paul's fellow laborers in the gospel of Christ. "Fellow laborers" means laborers together on the same plane and in the same work. This was only carrying out in a practical way the teaching of the Apostle that in Christ Jesus there is "neither male nor female."

In planting the gospel among different nations, varying in customs and social conditions, Paul on many occasions found it necessary as a matter of expediency to accommodate himself to particular social standards. (See I Cor. 9: 20-23.)

In this same epistle Paul admits that he wrote some things that were, in his opinion, "good for the present distress" (7:26); hence, were not a standard for all people and for all ages. One of the things to which he found it necessary to accommodate himself was the social standard concerning women in all provinces of the empire. The Corinthian church was in a heathen environment, to the social standards of which some deference had to be paid if the church hoped to win souls to

Christ. Women were regarded as vastly inferior to men and had no honorable place in the heathen religion; but, as Strabo informs us, one of their temples in Corinth had a thousand consecrated prostitutes. With such a social standard and such public sentiment concerning women's place in religion, what course could the Apostle take other than he did take—command the Christian women *there* to "keep silence in the churches" (14:34)?

The Work of the Church

The work of the church of God is twofold: (1) to care for and perpetuate itself; (2) to evangelize the world. It can prosper only as it keeps this twofold mission in view. A congregation that becomes self-centered, that cares for nothing but local prosperity, is almost sure to decline spiritually and miss its mission of assisting in carrying the gospel to a lost world. Missionary work was prominent in the apostolic church and was steadfastly pursued in obedience to Christ's command: "Go ye into all the world, and preach the gospel to every creature" (Mark 16:15). But the accomplishment of this great work required the sacrifice of men and of means. A noble army of consecrated men and women who "loved not their lives unto the death" went forth to struggle against the powers infernal and win the triumphs of the cross. The churches of God poured out their money in order to meet the demands of the hour, in some cases, as at Jerusalem, even selling their property and devoting the money to the interests of the cause of God.

The same spirit of self-denial and effort are needed today. The work of God needs men and women who are consecrated to evangelize the world, even at the cost of personal comforts and advantages; and the church of God must awaken to the fact that giving of means for the support of God's work is both a privilege and a duty, and that it must be done. "Even so hath the Lord ordained that they which preach the gospel should live of the gospel" (I Cor. 9:14). Those who minister to the people in "spiritual things" must receive the benefit of the people's "carnal things" (vs. 11). The work demands this; God demands it; and all the pure and holy in heart will say amen to the will of God.

Chapter 13

BAPTISM

The observance of ordinances in the New Testament church rests upon their institution by Christ and upon the last commission he gave to his apostles: "Go ye therefore, and teach all nations, baptizing them in the name of the Father, and of the Son, and of the Holy Ghost: teaching them to observe all things whatsoever I have commanded you: and, lo, I am with you alway, even unto the end of the world" (Matt. 28:19-20). In this text ordinances are expressly commanded, and their observance is to be perpetuated "unto the end of the world."

Some religious teachers oppose the observance of all ordinances, referring to Colossians 2:14 as proof that these were abolished at the death of Christ. But the text really shows that the abolished ordinances were those which belonged to the Mosaic law, for they are stated to be meats, drinks, holy days, new moons, and sabbaths (vss. 16-17). These were the "carnal ordinances, imposed on them until the time of reformation" (Heb. 9:10). "But Christ being come" (vs. 11), the reformation was brought in; the Mosaic institutions met their antitypes and thus were abolished through Christ's death; and the New Testament house, or church, of God, with its ordinances and institutions, succeeded.

This commission authorizing ministers to baptize was given after the death of Christ, and was consistently obeyed by the Apostles afterwards, as the Book of Acts abundantly shows. Some have affirmed that Paul did not believe in the ordinances, and therefore was quite indifferent to the subject at Corinth (see I Cor. 1:13-17), and that he baptized Crispus and Gaius and the household of Stephanus merely because they required it of him. But the inspired record shows that when Paul raised up this congregation "many of the Corinthians hearing, believed, and were baptized" (Acts 18:8). Now, if Paul himself did not do much of this baptizing, he had others do it, which shows his attitude toward baptism. Furthermore, he wrote to

99

this same congregation, "I have received of the Lord that which also I delivered unto you, That the Lord Jesus the same night in which he was betrayed took bread," referring to the ordinance of the Lord's Supper, as the context shows (I Cor. 11:23-28). Paul was not an antiordinance preacher.

It must also be borne in mind that Paul did not receive the gospel from those who were apostles before him, but by direct revelation from God, after the crucifixion and resurrection of Christ. (See Gal. 1:11-12, 15-17.) Where, then, did Paul get his authority to baptize and to observe the Lord's Supper? Not from the Apostles, but by the revelation of Jesus Christ— "for I have received of the Lord that which also I delivered unto you" (I Cor. 11:23). This proves positively that these ordinances were not abolished at the cross, for the Apostle was not even converted at the time of the crucifixion. Furthermore, the ordinances were not intended for the Jewish Christians only, because, as some assume, they loved ordinances so well; for Paul was specially commissioned to preach among the Gentiles (Acts 26:15-18).

A Believer's Baptism

The last commission of Christ, as recorded by Mark, is: "And he said unto them, Go ye into all the world, and preach the gospel to every creature. He that believeth and is baptized shall be saved; but he that believeth not shall be damned" (Mark 16:15-16). These words clearly limit the subjects of baptism to those who are capable of hearing and believing the gospel, and this standard was invariably maintained by the Apostles in their ministry. No children were baptized, only persons who believed—"men and women" (Acts 8:12).

The practice of giving a so-called baptism to young children originated in an apostate church. It is nowhere taught in the Bible, either by a single text or by a single example. Nor is infant baptism mentioned in any book until near the close of the second century, and then it was introduced as a result of two errors that were being taught: (1) That infants are totally depraved and therefore guilty and lost; (2) That baptism itself regenerates from sin. When men believed these two false doctrines, they baptized infants as the only means of removing their depravity and preventing their going to hell in case of death.

There is no valid reason for the observance of this infant rite. The often repeated statement that the Apostles must have baptized infants, because they sometimes baptized households, has no weight; for there is no proof in a single instance that there were infants in these households. Furthermore, in most cases, the context itself shows that believers only were baptized. For examples, see the records concerning the household of Cornelius (Acts 10) and the household of the jailer (16: 31-34). Baptism is "the answer of a good conscience toward God" (I Pet. 3:21), but conscience is not operative in infants.

Nor does this rite of infant baptism decrease in any sense the parental obligation to endeavor to "bring them up in the nurture and admonition of the Lord." No good can possibly come to infants by this unscriptural rite; on the contrary, an incalculable amount of harm results. One writer urges infant baptism in order that the children "should never be allowed to believe that they were naturally aliens from the household of faith." This is the very harm that comes through infant baptism; for at this very day millions who were baptized (?) in infancy believe that they have always been the children of God, though they have never been "born again" and are really in a lost condition.

It is not the so-called act of baptism itself that is so harmful; it is the accompanying belief that those so baptized are Christians from their infancy. This belief is especially strong in the East, where all baptized people (irrespective of moral character) are called Christians, and those who have not had the rite are, by the so-called Christians, generally termed heathen. The doctrine of Christ is that "except a man be born again, he cannot see the kingdom of God" (John 3:3). "He that believeth and is baptized shall be saved." When saved from their sins they should then be "baptized, both men and women" (Acts 8:12).

Conditioned on Repentance

"In those days came John the Baptist, preaching . . . and saying, Repent ye: for the kingdom of heaven is at hand. . . .

Then went out to him Jerusalem, and all Judea, and all the
region round about Jordan, and were baptized of him in Jordan, confessing their sins" (Matt. 3:1-2, 5-6). Not only did John
teach that the people should repent and then be baptized, but
he actually required repentance of them, refusing to baptize
them if they did not repent (vss. 7-8). We read in another place
that "the Pharisees and lawyers rejected the counsel of God
against themselves, being not baptized of him" (Luke 7:30).
Because of their unwillingness to meet the required conditions
for baptism, it is said that they "rejected the counsel of God."
And so it is with all antiordinance people; by rejecting Bible
baptism they are rejecting God's Word.

In his Pentecostal sermon Peter taught the same truth concerning the necessity of repentance first and baptism afterwards: "Repent, and be baptized every one of you" (Acts 2:38).
Unless the heart is brought into the right attitude through repentance, the simple act of baptism amounts to nothing, even
though performed in the Bible manner and by a true minister
of God. Simon the sorcerer, at Samaria, was baptized with the
other believers; yet when Peter and John came down, the un-
regenerate condition of the man's heart was revealed. His baptism in water, even though performed by Philip, a man "filled
with the Holy Ghost," did not take away from his heart the
love of pre-eminence, which had possessed him in the past.
Peter said to him plainly, "Thou hast neither part nor lot in
this matter: for thy heart is not right in the sight of God"
(8:21).

Baptism as a Burial

The mode of baptism has been a much-debated subject. But
consideration of a few Scripture passages should be sufficient
to show that immersion is the Bible mode of baptism. In fact,
almost without exception, theologians admit the validity of
immersion; the chief controversy has arisen over the effort on
the part of many to prove that sprinkling or pouring may be
substituted for it.

All scholars admit that "to immerse" is the plain English
equivalent of the Greek word *baptizo*. "Sprinkle" and "pour"
are not equivalent to "immerse," as the lexicons testify. Three
words in the Greek language are equivalent respectively to

the three English words "immerse," "sprinkle," and "pour."
Now, whenever the Bible speaks of baptism as a literal Christian rite, it always employs the Greek word that is the equivalent of the English word "immersion." If the Bible writers, using Greek, desired to convey the idea of "pour," why did they not use the Greek word that signifies "pour," instead of the word that signifies "immerse"? or use a word for "sprinkle" if they meant "sprinkle"? The reason is evident: they said what they meant, and, I may add, meant what they said.

This distinction is so clear that wherever the literal Christian rite is spoken of one can substitute "immerse" or "immersion" without in any degree changing the meaning; whereas, in many cases if we substitute "sprinkle" or "pour" the passage is made ridiculous. (See, e.g., Acts 8:36-39; Col. 2:12.) There is no mention of sprinkling or pouring for baptism until near the close of the second century, when it was introduced in case of sickness and was not regarded as regular. Furthermore, all the facts and circumstances concerning baptism recorded in the New Testament harmonize with the mode of immersion, but not on any other supposition.

The great historians, as Neander, Mosheim, Wall, Weiss, Ewald, Geikie, Edersheim, De Pressense, Conybeare, Stanley, Schaff, and many others, testify that immersion was the primitive practice. This was also affirmed by the great reformers.

Baptism is a ceremonial representation of the burial and resurrection of our Lord; therefore, only immersion is appropriate. In fact, the individual believer symbolically follows Christ in his death, burial, and resurrection. First he dies the death to sin, is "crucified with Christ" (Gal. 2:20); then he is "buried with him in baptism, wherein also ye are risen with him through the faith of the operation of God, who hath raised him from the dead" (Col. 2:12). Baptism thus becomes to the individual an outward sign of an inward work. First we are "circumcised with the circumcision made without hands, in putting off the body of the sins of the flesh" (vs. 11); then we are "buried with him in baptism."

The same idea is alluded to in that remarkable passage in Romans 6:2, 4: "How shall we that are dead to sin live any longer therein? . . . Therefore we are buried with him by baptism into death: that like as Christ was raised up from the dead by the glory of the Father, even so we also should walk in newness of life."

Christ was buried in baptism. John was baptizing "in Jordan" (Mark 1:5). "Then cometh Jesus from Galilee to Jordan unto John, to be baptized of him. . . . And Jesus, when he was baptized, went up straightway out of the water: and, lo, the heavens were opened unto him, and he saw the Spirit of God descending like a dove, and lighting upon him: and lo a voice from heaven, saying, This is my beloved Son, in whom I am well pleased" (Matt. 3:13, 16-17). Jesus evidently went down into the Jordan in order to be baptized, for after his baptism, he "went up straightway out of the water." Here we have the highest authority for immersion in water, which is thus known to be Heaven's plan: (1) *Jesus himself,* the Son of God, set the example (that of itself should be sufficient); (2) *the Holy Spirit,* the third person in the Trinity, bore witness by appearing visibly in the form of a dove and lighting upon Christ; (3) *the Father* declared in audible tones, "I am well pleased."

In order to fulfill the Word of God perfectly and secure a valid baptism the candidate must observe the following:

1. *He must know or hear the gospel* (Mark 16:15).

2. *He must repent of his sins and believe the gospel,* the doing of which will bring about his salvation (Acts 3:19; 16:31; 2:38).

3. *He must find a minister of God who is ready to baptize him.* (See Acts 8:36-37.)

4. *Preacher and candidate must go to a place where there is "much water"* (John 3:23).

5. *Then he must follow the example of Christ* in his baptism (Matt. 3:16), by going down "into the water." (See Acts 8:38).

6. *Then he must be "buried . . . in baptism."*

7. *The candidate can then "come up out of the water"* (Acts 8:39).

8. Then, having obeyed the Word and followed his Lord, *he can go "on his way rejoicing"* (Acts 8:39).

Reader, have you met the required conditions and been baptized in this Bible way? If not, you have not been baptized at all; nothing short of this constitutes scriptural, valid baptism.

Single Immersion

From the formula given by Jesus—"Baptizing them in the name of the Father, and of the Son, and of the Holy Ghost" (Matt. 28:19)—some have inferred that a threefold action is necessary—one immersion in the name of the Father, one in the name of the Son, and one in the name of the Holy Ghost. In the Acts of the Apostles this threefold formula is never mentioned; the people were simply baptized "in the name of Jesus Christ," or "in the name of the Lord," or "in the name of the Lord Jesus" (Acts 2:38; 8:16; 10:48; 19:5), which shows that the Apostles did not understand that it was necessary to perform a triple action. The Father, Son, and Holy Ghost are one; therefore one action is sufficient.

Furthermore, the object and design of baptism preclude the idea of repetition. It is the outward sign of an inward work, representing our salvation from sin. Now, this salvation is represented as the work *of God* (II Tim. 1:8-9), as the work *of Christ* (Matt. 1:21), and as the work *of the Holy Spirit* (John 3:5); yet it is *a single act,* and, therefore, can be appropriately represented only by a *single immersion* in the threefold name, just as truly as the single conversion is the work of the divine Trinity. If we were converted three times, once by each person of the Trinity, then triune immersion in three separate names would properly represent it. So also the symbolic reference baptism bears to the burial, and resurrection of Christ necessitates the single action. Christ was buried once and raised once; and we are "buried with him [once] in baptism" and "are risen [once] with him" to "walk in newness of life."

Baptism as a Purifying Ordinance

To the Jewish mind baptism appealed very strongly as a purifying ordinance. The Jews had long been accustomed to "divers washings" of a ceremonial nature, and on this account were led to regard baptism in a similar light. Therefore, when John came baptizing in Enon near Salim, presenting a new cleansing ceremony, straightway "there arose a question between some of John's disciples and the Jews about purifying" (John 3:23-25).

The Apostles also presented the subject in the light of a purifying ordinance. Peter said to the penitent Jews, "Repent, and be baptized every one of you in the name of Jesus Christ, for the remission of sins" (Acts 2:38). The language implies that baptism, as well as repentance, is for the remission of sins. So also Ananias said to Saul, "And now why tarriest thou? arise, and be baptized, and wash away thy sins, calling on the name of the Lord" (22:16).

The Jews were accustomed to the idea of double cleansing— actual and ceremonial. By consulting Leviticus 14:2-7, where the law concerning the cleansing of the leper is given, the reader will see that the actual healing of the leper is one thing and that his ceremonial "cleansing" is another thing. This double cleansing was recognized by Christ; for when he granted a leper perfect healing (the actual work), he said to him, "Go thy way, show thyself to the priest, and offer the [ceremonial] gift that Moses commanded, for a testimony unto them" (Matt. 8:4).

Now, baptism as a purifying ordinance does not cleanse the soul from sin actually, but ceremonially, being "a testimony unto them"—the people. It is the outward sign of an inward work of grace. We are "dead to sin," "therefore buried with him by baptism" (Rom. 6:2, 4). The actual cleansing of the soul from sinful elements cannot be effected by literal water; it is "the blood of Christ" that is able to "purge your conscience from dead works to serve the living God" (Heb. 9:14). Yea, "he hath washed us from our sins in his own blood" (Rev. 1:5). "The blood of Jesus Christ his Son cleanseth us from all sin" (I John 1:7).

Peter also shows the figurative nature of baptismal cleansing, or salvation. (See I Pet. 3:20-21.) Baptism is not our actual salvation, but our figurative one; it is not the actual "putting away of the filth of the flesh, but the answer of a good conscience toward God." How do we obtain this good conscience? The blood of Christ purifies our conscience (Heb. 9:14). Therefore we have blood cleansing first, and ceremonial, or water, cleansing afterwards, as the "answer of a good conscience toward God."

Chapter 14

THE LORD'S SUPPER

The New Testament teaches the observance of an ordinance termed "the Lord's Supper." This expression, however, is used only once: "When ye come together therefore into one place, this is not to eat the Lord's supper" (I Cor. 11:20). As there has been considerable misunderstanding regarding this ordinance, I shall refer to what the Bible really teaches concerning it.

Not a Regular Meal

The Corinthian church, it appears, misunderstood this subject, and in Paul's absence they either substituted something else for the Lord's Supper or else added something to the proper rite; therefore Paul wrote to them for the purpose of correcting the matter. (See I Cor. 11:20-22.)

They were coming together for a full meal, very much like the idolatrous feasts of the heathen in that city, and their excesses on these occasions were a reproach to the church of God. Paul severely condemned them for this practice, declaring that their coming together for a full meal, or feast, was not "the Lord's supper," but was only their "own supper"; that the proper place for eating their own supper was in their own houses, not in the church of God. "If any man hunger," he wrote, "let him eat at home; that ye come not together into condemnation" (vs. 34).

A Commemorative Institution

Paul then proceeded to show what the true Lord's Supper really is: "For I have received of the Lord that which also I delivered unto you, That the Lord Jesus the same night in which he was betrayed took bread: and when he had given thanks, he brake it, and said, Take, eat: this is my body, which is broken for you: this do in remembrance of me. After the same manner also he took the cup, when he had supped, say-

107

ing, This cup is the new testament in my blood: this do ye, as oft as ye drink it, in remembrance of me. For as often as ye eat this bread, and drink this cup, ye do show the Lord's death till he come" (I Cor. 11:23-26).

According to the Apostle, the Lord's Supper is the eating of the bread and the drinking of the cup, after the example set by Christ. Therefore, the Lord's Supper and the Communion are the same (I Cor. 10:16).

Now, as Paul states, this ordinance was instituted by Christ himself. "And as they were eating, Jesus took bread, and blessed it, and brake it, and gave it to the disciples, and said, Take, eat; this is my body. And he took the cup, and gave thanks, and gave it to them, saying, Drink ye all of it, for this is my blood of the new testament, which is shed for many for the remission of sins" (Matt. 26:26-28).

Following the example and commandment of Christ, the apostolic church observed the ordinance (Acts 20:7). The testimony of the earliest Church Fathers is to the effect that this ordinance was observed regularly by all Christians; and the observance has continued among true Christians until the present day.

The Purpose of the Communion Service

The Communion has an object and is intended to teach something, for Christ would not establish an ordinance in his church without a distinct purpose in view. Much of the original design, however, has been lost or obscured by the accumulation of human rubbish in the form of mystical theological opinions and false notions. For instance, the Roman Catholics teach that the bread and wine are, at the time of consecration, converted into the actual body and blood of Christ. But my purpose is not to show what the Roman Catholics teach, nor what the Greek church teaches, nor what Protestant denominations teach and believe: it is to show *what the Bible teaches.*

The special design of this ordinance is shown in the words of Christ when commanding its observance: "This do in remembrance of me" (Luke 22:19). If the ordinance is "in remembrance" of Christ, then it is not actually Christ himself (though it symbolically represents him in his atonement), but is a commemorative institution by which the sufferings of Christ for our sins are brought vividly before our minds, and we are brought into closer fellowship with his sufferings and death. "For as often as ye eat this bread, and drink this cup, ye do show the Lord's death till he come" (I Cor. 11:26). In observing it, we do not obtain spiritual life, but we "show the Lord's death."

"Wherefore whosoever shall eat this bread, and drink this cup of the Lord, unworthily, shall be guilty of the body and blood of the Lord. But let a man examine himself, and so let him eat of that bread, and drink of that cup. For he that eateth and drinketh unworthily, eateth and drinketh damnation to himself, not discerning the Lord's body" (I Cor. 11:27-29). People who do not discern the Lord's body—his sacrificial body—in its true character as a sin offering, and who are not thereby actually redeemed from their sins, are unworthy to partake of this ordinance which "shows the Lord's death"; therefore, if they "eat this bread and drink this cup," they are "guilty of the body and blood of the Lord"; they eat and drink damnation to themselves.

While the Lord's Supper is commemorative of the sufferings and death of our Lord, representing symbolically his crucified body, it also has another important signification: it represents the collective and unified body of believers in Christ. "The cup of blessing which we bless, is it not the communion of the blood of Christ? The bread which we break, is it not the communion of the body of Christ? For we [saved believers] being many are one bread, and one body; for we are all partakers of that one bread" (I Cor. 10:16-17).

In its unbroken state the loaf of bread used in the Communion service represents very beautifully the one body of saved believers. The flour out of which it is made was ground from many kernels of wheat, which possibly were grown in many separate fields; yet all these grains have been brought together and by a certain process have been unified in one loaf—even their nature has been changed by the process of baking. So also God's true and redeemed saints are many and they have been widely separated; yet through Christ they have been "perfectly joined together" by his Holy Spirit, their natures have been changed from sin to holiness, and they are indeed "all one in Christ Jesus." The one loaf properly represents their unity in the body of Jesus Christ—his church.

The Perpetuity of the Lord's Supper

That the ordinance of the Lord's Supper was intended to be observed throughout the Christian dispensation is made clear by the Scriptures themselves. We have already seen that it was observed in the apostolic church. Christ commissioned his ministers to go and "teach all nations." Teach them what? "To observe all things whatsoever I have commanded you" (Matt. 28:19-20). Did he command the observance of the Lord's Supper? "This do in remembrance of me" (Luke 22:19). How long was this to continue? "Teaching them to observe all things whatsoever I have commanded you: and, lo, I am with you alway, even unto the end of the world" (Matt. 28:20).

This is clear. So long as the gospel is to be preached, just so long the people are to observe all things that Christ commanded—"even unto the end of the world." So also we read in another place, "For as often as ye eat this bread, and drink this cup, ye do show the Lord's death till he come" (I Cor. 11:26). Then, it is to be observed by the true followers of Christ in all periods of the Christian dispensation, till he comes again.

Chapter 15

FOOT WASHING

In our day most professing Christians do not rank foot washing as an ordinance of the church. They generally insist on observing baptism and the Lord's Supper, but they pass by foot washing in complete silence, as if the subject were not so much as mentioned in the Word of God. Our purpose, however, is not to write a history of Christianity, nor to chronicle the development of technical theology, with its diverse standards of ritualistic church observances; it is to narrate clearly and plainly what the Bible teaches.

Jesus instructed his first apostles to teach all nations to observe all things whatsoever I have commanded you" (Matt. 28:20). Did he command foot washing as one of the "all things"? Let the Bible answer.

"And supper being ended, the devil having now put into the heart of Judas Iscariot, Simon's son, to betray him; Jesus knowing that the Father had given all things into his hands, and that he was come from God, and went to God; he riseth from supper, and laid aside his garments; and took a towel, and girded himself. After that he poureth water into a basin, and began to wash the disciples' feet, and to wipe them with the towel wherewith he was girded. Then cometh he to Simon Peter: and Peter saith unto him, Lord, dost thou wash my feet? Jesus answered and said unto him, What I do thou knowest not now; but thou shalt know hereafter. Peter saith unto him, Thou shalt never wash my feet. Jesus answered him, If I wash thee not, thou hast no part with me. Simon Peter saith unto him, Lord, not my feet only, but also my hands and my head. Jesus saith unto him, He that is washed needeth not save to wash his feet, but is clean every whit: and ye are clean, but not all. For he knew who should betray him; therefore said he, Ye are not all clean. So after he had washed their feet, and had taken his garments, and was set down again, he said unto them, Know ye what I have done to you? Ye call me Master and Lord: and ye say well; for so I am. If I then, your Lord and Master, have washed your feet; ye also ought to wash one another's feet. For I have given you an example, that ye should do as I have done to you. Verily, verily, I say unto you, The servant is not greater than his lord; neither he that is sent greater than he that sent him. If ye know these things, happy are ye if ye do them" (John 13:2-17).

Expressly Commanded

[handwritten: Literal interpretation] By the foregoing we see that foot washing is expressly commanded and that at the very least it must be practiced in some form.

Some say that this part of the Word does not assert that we *must* do it, but merely that we *should* or *ought*. Now, the New Testament law of liberty does not consist of "thou shalt," as did the Mosaic law, but is, instead, a law of love, and Jesus says, "If a man love me, he will keep my words" (John 14:23). The true, humblehearted Christian needs no further coercion than the simple knowledge that he "ought" to do a thing, yea, "should" do it. These are the strongest words in our language expressing moral obligation or duty, as everyone must admit. Their true application and force are admitted in every other case where they are employed: for example: "Men ought always to pray" (Luke 18:1). "We ought to obey God" (Acts 5:29). "So ought men to love their wives as their own bodies" (Eph. 5:28). (See also I John 3:23; 4:11.)

Men may try to explain away these words of Christ; they may substitute something else for this ordinance or call it nonessential, but still Christ's words remain: "Ye also ought to wash one another's feet"; "Do as I have done to you."

Scriptural Symbols

In a pamphlet *The Ordinance We Forget,* Dr. Charles Ewing Brown says of symbols in the ancient Christian church:

"There are some symbols ordained by Scripture which I am sure we ought to hold in everlasting remembrance. These symbols are often called sacraments. Of these different churches give a different number. The Church of Rome counts seven. Most Protestants hold only two. . . .

"How many symbols of the Christian life were ordained by Christ? Not only two, but three, as every reader of the New Testament knows. Christ ordained and directed us to perform three separate acts of our religion—baptism, the Lord's Supper, and foot washing. *All Christians acknowledge this.*"

The Purpose of Ordinances

The specific purpose of foot washing as an ordinance is closely bound up with the basic reasons underlying the other two ordinances of the church. But why ordinances at all, one might ask? We ought to be willing to obey plain commandments of our Lord, just because he is the Lord, whether or not we can discern the reasons for such commands. Still, numerous reasons are evident for the observance of church ordinances. For example, by requiring actual association and fellowship with others of like faith, Christian ordinances, literally observed, prevent Christianity from becoming purely and exclusively individualistic.

1. *Baptism,* as a public Christian act, forms and assures a visible break with the past and becomes the outward sign of identification with the Christian church and community. It is therefore a visible testimony to the world.

2. *The Lord's Supper.* This ordinance, which is often repeated, requires the frequent association and constant group fellowship of the people of God and, as a memorial of Christ's sacrificial death, symbolizes specifically our relations to God as constant and permanent "till he come."

3. *Foot washing.* As a Christian ordinance, foot washing symbolizes, as does nothing else, the sacredness and holiness of that blessed *relationship of God's redeemed saints with each other.*

If spiritual separation from the world, as a distinct act of God's grace, demands outward expression and exhibition in Christian baptism; if the moral and inner secret of regeneration through the atonement and our abiding life in Christ calls for outward and frequent expression in the literal observance of the Lord's Supper; then, and equally true and important, that inner and spiritual relationship of brother to brother—real, God-given, divine—calls for a corresponding outward expression such as Christ himself instituted when he said, "Wash one another's feet."

Practiced in the Apostolic Church

First, as we have seen, Christ himself set the example, instituted the practice, and then commanded its observance. That is sufficient to establish it; for it is exactly the same method by which the other two ordinances were established. It is not mentioned many times in the New Testament, but why should it be? Must the command of Christ be repeated over and over in order to make it authoritative? The new birth is set forth clearly only in the same Gospel, that of John, in the conversation Christ held with Nicodemus; yet this doctrine is all-important—the very foundation of true Christianity itself. So also the Communion service, observed in some form by nearly all Christians, is mentioned only twice in the Epistles (I Cor. 10:16; 11:20-34); yet no one denies that it was generally observed in the apostolic church.

The Apostles preached the whole gospel message in the churches that they raised up; hence, when they wrote letters to them afterwards they had no reason for setting forth doctrine specifically, unless conditions required it. It will be seen, therefore, that the doctrine set forth in these epistles occurs rather by accident—one might say, the result of circumstances. It is not at all likely that Paul would have mentioned the Communion in his letter to the Corinthians had it not been for the misunderstanding and perversion of the ordinance that existed there. Foot washing is mentioned in the same casual way—but it is mentioned. Writing to Timothy relative to certain conditions under which a widow should be taken under the financial care of the church, Paul says she should be "well reported of for good works; if she have brought up children, if she have lodged strangers, if she have washed the saints' feet, if she have relieved the afflicted, if she have diligently followed every good work" (I Tim. 5:10).

The fact that this service was extended only to "the saints" is evidence that it was no ordinary act of regular duty or hospitality. but that it possessed a religious and churchly significance. Christ apparently attached religious significance to foot washing when he first established it; for he said to Peter, the first Christian to object to the practice, "If I wash thee not, thou hast no part with me" (John 13:8).

Tertullian mentions foot washing as being observed by Christians in his day. So also Augustine, a little later. Its practice in Gaul, Spain, and Italy is also a matter of historic record. In fact, the oldest churches, such as the Greek, the Roman Catholic, and the Gregorian (Armenian), have retained the rite in their religious systems until the present day. There is no reasonable way to account for the origin of this practice among these old and independent churches except by acknowledging that it was the practice of the original church. True, they have peculiar ways of observing it, but they have perverted the other ordinances as well; yet they keep them all in some form or other.

Let me ask in all candor, Can such an ordinance as foot washing, literally observed and commanded by our Lord, and literally practiced by millions of Christians from apostolic times until today, possibly be wrong?

"Ye call me Master and Lord: and ye say well; for so I am. If I then, your Lord and Master, have washed your feet; ye also ought to wash one another's feet. For I have given you an example, that ye should do as I have done to you. . . . If ye know these things, happy are ye if ye do them" (John 13:13-17).

What It Teaches Us

The ordinance of foot washing, like the other ordinances, is intended to teach us some important lessons. In the first place, it teaches a real lesson of humility, made very clear to us when we undertake to practice it. It sets forth our position of equality in the church, showing that we all, as brethren and sisters, belong on the same common level. Jesus himself, our Lord and Master, humbled himself and washed the feet of his disciples; therefore, how much more reasonable it is that we should wash one another's feet. It also shows that we are properly servants of each other, that we must minister to the good of each other. In practicing it, however, we must observe the proper sex distinctions, as recognized by society. "Let all things be done decently and in order" (I Cor. 14:40).

Oh, how real this all becomes when we humbly obey the Word! "If ye know these things, happy are ye if ye do them." In the last great day our Lord will say, "As ye have done it unto one of the least of these my brethren, ye have done it unto me" (Matt. 25:40).

Some Objections Considered

One objection, frequently urged, is that foot washing is not mentioned very often in the New Testament. This has been sufficiently considered already under the subhead "Practiced in the Apostolic Church." Another objection is in the form of the "sandal" theory.

According to the "sandal" theory, Christ washed his disciples' feet for the purpose of cleanliness because they wore sandals and had been traveling a dusty road. But the custom of sandal wearing is still in existence in the Orient, and while personally engaged in missionary work there I have been unable to find that it is a custom for the people to "wash one another's feet." Furthermore, I have observed that those religious people who claim that Christ washed the disciples' feet because wearing sandals made cleansing necessary, do not obey the injunction, "Wash one another's feet," when engaged in missionary work among these sandal-wearing people. If the foot washing that Christ performed and commanded was founded on sandal wearing, why do they not obey it, at least in the same country and under the same conditions?

"If I then, your Lord and Master, have washed your feet; ye also ought to wash one another's feet."

CONCERNING THE CHURCH IN PROPHECY AND HISTORY

Chapter 16

THE APOSTOLIC PERIOD

In previous chapters I have given a brief description of the establishment of the church of God in the Apostolic Age, showing its divine organization and characteristics. This description was drawn principally from the Gospels, the Acts of the Apostles, and some of the epistles of Paul. But the mission of the church was not to be limited to the period of the Apostles; it was designed to be world-wide in its extent and to be perpetual, "even unto the end of the world." This being the case, it was fitting that the history of the church should be described prophetically, in order that we might have definite knowledge concerning the operations of the Divine Hand in working out the church's destiny after the close of the sacred canon.

Preliminary Statement

We must not overlook the particular place and the supreme importance of *prophecy* in the divine plan. In the Old Testament dispensation prophets of God predicted many things which came to pass soon in current Hebrew history, but they also uttered many Messianic prophecies, which were to meet their fulfillment in a new and better dispensation. And in the New Testament we read over and over again, "It came to pass that it might be fulfilled which was spoken by the prophet." The Apostle Paul declares that the church of God itself is "built upon the foundation of the apostles and prophets" (Eph. 2:20). The church, built upon prophets, as we are told, was also to be graced by the presence and work of prophets of God. "God hath set some in the church, first apostles, secondarily prophets" (I Cor. 12:28). "When he ascended up on high he . . . gave gifts unto men. And he gave some . . .

117

prophets . . . for the edifying of the body of Christ" (Eph. 4:8, 11-12). Paul and Peter, as outstanding prophets in the early church, predicted many things that would take place later in the history of God's unfolding work, but in the Seer of Patmos apocalyptic vision reached supreme heights, carrying forward the history of God's church through four distinct and well-defined periods, or epochs, reaching to the end of time itself and to the introduction of the last things.

Purpose and Limitations of This Prophetic Sketch

The field of prophecy is so vast that in the limits of space consistent with the main purpose of this book I can do no more than give the briefest sketch. Neither involved questions of interpretation nor minor details can be discussed.

The general method of prophetic treatment employed may be described as evangelical and orthodox. In recent years there has come into some prominence a group of so-called interpreters who question or deny altogether the divine element in our holy religion; who neither believe in divine revelation itself, in miracles, nor in true predictive prophecy. To these—and to a few others who are more or less influenced by their theories —the Book of Revelation is regarded as having no true prophetic value applying to the unfolding of historic events throughout this dispensation; it is classed by them as but another example of the apocalyptic literature rather common in those early days, being nothing but veiled allusions to current events.

The vast majority of commentators and interpreters—including most of the greatest scholars and the noblest Christians who have ever graced the Christian church—have firmly believed in the validity of prophecy and, notwithstanding great variety in their individual interpretations, have generally regarded the prophecies of Revelation as applicable to actual unfolding events in history, to be climaxed finally by the second coming and the last things. I feel honored to stand in their company.

Naturally, I hesitate about applying important symbols to particular events or times when, under the space limitations,

I am unable to bring forward satisfactory and convincing proofs.*

With this apology for a partial and inconclusive treatment of an otherwise entrancing and inspiring subject, I shall proceed with the sketch.

With the breaking forth of the glorious light of pristine Christianity arose the church of God, established in unity and in purity, glorious in power, and adorned with all the rich graces of the Holy Spirit. Who can describe her? "Her ways are ways of pleasantness, and all her paths are peace" (Prov. 3:17). She is the bride of Christ (John 3:29), the heavenly Jerusalem (Rev. 21:9-10 with Heb. 12:22-23), which is "the mother of us all" (Gal. 4:26).

The Symbolic Woman

John saw her in apocalyptic vision, and he describes her thus: "And there appeared a great wonder in heaven; a woman clothed with the sun, and the moon under her feet, and upon her head a crown of twelve stars: and she being with child cried, travailing in birth, and pained to be delivered" (Rev. 12:1-2).

The woman appears as the symbol of the church of God in its early glory. She was arrayed in the most splendid manner, all the brightest luminaries of heaven being gathered around her, thus symbolizing the divine light and glory and exaltation of the primitive church. But she had enemies.

"And there appeared another wonder in heaven; and behold a great red dragon, having seven heads and ten horns, and seven crowns upon his heads. And his tail drew the third part of the stars of heaven, and did cast them to the earth: and the dragon stood before the woman which was ready to be delivered, for to devour her child as soon as it was born. And she brought forth a man-child, who was to rule all nations with a rod of iron: and her child was caught up unto God, and to his

*The prophecies pertaining specifically to the church, briefly alluded to in the present sketch, are treated thoroughly by the author in his book *Prophetic Lectures on Daniel and the Revelation*. To those who are interested in the general field of prophecy, or in the entire Book of Revelation in particular, my well-known commentary, *The Revelation Explained*, will be found to contain an adequate and satisfactory treatment of the subject, based on a sound foundation laid down in the introductory chapter, entitled "The Nature of Symbolic Language." That book may be secured from the publishers of this work.

throne. And the woman fled into the wilderness, where she
hath a place prepared of God, that they should feed her there
a thousand two hundred and threescore days" (vss. 3-6).

In the Revelation, symbols drawn from the department of
human life invariably refer to ecclesiastical affairs, whereas
those drawn from the natural world or inanimate nature usually refer to civil or political affairs, and thus a proper cor-
respondence of character and quality is kept up.

The Great Dragon

The dragon of this vision, if such a creature actually existed,
would be a beast from the natural world; therefore it properly
symbolizes a tyrannical, persecuting power or government.
This we must identify in order to understand the nature of the
opposition to the woman, the church.

It was a "red dragon, having seven heads and ten horns, and
seven crowns upon his heads." In the following chapter (Rev.
13) we read that John saw a beast rising up out of the sea
with the same number of heads and horns, but ten crowns on
his horns. "And the dragon gave him [the beast] his power,
and his seat, and great authority" (vs. 2). So far as the heads
and the horns are concerned, the only difference between the
two is that the crowns—a symbol of supreme authority and
power—have been transferred from the heads to the horns.
John saw the same beast again and received the following
explanation of the seven heads: "And there are seven kings:
five are fallen, and one is, and the other is not yet come; and
when he cometh he must continue a short space" (17:10). Concerning the horns he was told, "The ten horns which thou
sawest are ten kings, which have received no kingdom as yet"
(vs. 12).

With this explanation before us, it will be easy to identify
the dragon of chapter 12 and the beast of chapters 13 and 17 as
the Roman Empire; the first under the pagan form, and the
second under the papal. The seven heads signify the seven
distinct forms of supreme government that ruled successively
in the empire. The five that had already fallen when John received the vision were the regal power, the consular, the de-
cemvirate, the military tribunes, and the triumvirate. "One is"

—the imperial. The ten horns, or kingdoms, which had not yet risen when the Revelation was given, were the ten minor kingdoms that grew out of the Western Roman Empire during its decline and fall.

The dragon is described with the horns, although they were not yet in existence and did not rise until near the time when the dragon became the beast, as we shall see later. Likewise, he is represented with seven heads, although he really possessed only one head at a time, and five had already fallen, and one was yet to come. He is described with all the heads and horns that he ever had and was to have.

This description is not literal, as some people imagine, but is symbolic. And with our knowledge of the proper use of symbols, we can easily identify this dragon with the Roman Empire under its pagan form.

The Man-Child

A careful study of the facts brought out in the New Testament shows that the man-child symbolizes the mighty host of new converts, or children, that the early church by her earnest travail brought forth. There is also a distinct reason why the church of God in this dispensation should be represented by two individuals—a woman and her son. If but a single symbol were used, how could the church be thereby represented as continuing on earth and fleeing into the wilderness, and at the same time be represented as "overcome," persecuted to the death, and "caught up unto God and to his throne"?

The Scriptures also testify concerning the identity of this man-child in Isaiah 66:7-8. According to Hebrews 12:22-23, this Zion, or Sion, is the New Testament church, and the man-child that she is said to bring forth is interpreted by Isaiah as "a nation . . . born at once." Such language perfectly describes the rapid increase in the church on Pentecost and shortly afterwards, when thousands were added in one day. According to Paul, the host of Jews and Gentiles reconciled to God through Jesus Christ constituted "one new man" in Christ Jesus (Eph. 2:15. See also Gal. 3:28, ASV.)

The Holy War

"And there was war in heaven: Michael and his angels fought against the dragon; and the dragon fought and his angels, and prevailed not; neither was their place found any more in heaven. And the great dragon was cast out, that old serpent, called the Devil, and Satan, which deceiveth the whole world: he was cast out into the earth, and his angels were cast out with him. And I heard a loud voice saying in heaven, Now is come salvation, and strength, and the kingdom of our God, and the power of his Christ: for the accuser of our brethren is cast down, which accused them before our God day and night. And they overcame him by the blood of the Lamb, and by the word of their testimony; and they loved not their lives unto the death" (Rev. 12:7-11).

This was not a literal conflict fought in the real heaven, as some imaginative writers and orators have pictured; it was a conflict symbolically pictured in heaven, but which actually took place upon the earth.

The whole scene is highly symbolic of the fierce conflict that took place between the early followers of Christ and the hosts of paganism; and so sweeping was the victory gained by the soldiers of the cross that the cry was heard, "Now is come salvation, and strength, and the kingdom of our God, and the power of his Christ; for the accuser of our brethren is cast down, which accused them before our God day and night."

The fact that so many Christians lost their lives in this conflict (vs. 11), that the man-child is represented as caught up to God (vs. 5), shows that the dragon employed also the arm of civil power in his opposition to the growing truth. But Christianity increased rapidly, notwithstanding the violent opposition and persecutions by the pagans. An example of its progress is given in Acts 19 where it is said that the entire city of Ephesus was stirred over the preaching of Paul. Before the death of the last of the Apostles, according to the younger Pliny, the temples of the gods in Asia Minor were almost forsaken. In this golden period the true church of God shone forth in all her glory and beauty.

Chapter 17

THE GREAT APOSTASY

The pure church of the apostolic period was not to continue ever with glories undimmed. It was God's will that she should remain the same, but conditions among men were destined to bring about a great change in her spiritual affairs; therefore, inspiration has given us in advance a description of the great Apostasy. (See II Pet. 2:1-2; Matt. 24:12.)

A Falling Away

Paul gives us a particular description of the Apostasy. To the Thessalonians he says concerning the second coming of Christ, "Let no man deceive you by any means: for that day shall not come, except there come a falling away first, and that man of sin be revealed, the son of perdition; who opposeth and exalteth himself above all that is called God, or that is worshiped; so that he as God sitteth in the temple of God, showing himself that he is God" (II Thess. 2:3-4).

By consulting the historical facts we find that these predictions were only too true. Even before the death of the Apostles themselves the Apostasy was beginning to work. In the seven churches in Asia Minor, addressed in Revelation 2—3 we find proof of this sad deflection.

The Apostasy Universal

Now the history of the church since it first became extensive has always been interwoven with the political affairs of nations and kingdoms. In the early ages its expansion was practically limited to the boundaries of the Roman Empire; therefore, its development and character were largely bound up with the fortunes of that empire itself. From the time of the permanent separation of the empire into eastern and western divisions, the churches of the East and the West gradually became more and more separated from each other and were designated by the term "Greek" in the East and "Latin" in the West, on account of the prevailing languages. Finally, the rupture became complete.

We must remember that before this separation took place, and while the churches East and West were closely united, the great Apostasy set in and affected the church universal. Therefore, since the separation we have simply two great divisions of the one great apostasy. Out of the one division developed the churches of the East—Greek, Old Syrian, Gregorian (Armenian), Abyssinian, Nestorian, Coptic, and others; while from the other divisions arose the Papacy in the West, and out of it Protestantism with its many divisions, as we shall see presently. Since the fortunes of the West, political and ecclesiastical, were destined to rise to greater heights and to overshadow and eclipse the fortunes of the East, the prophecies are naturally directed more particularly to the Western Empire, bringing into prominence the development of ecclesiasticism.

The Papacy

In the passage already quoted—II Thessalonians 2:3-4—it is the Papacy that the Apostle so graphically describes, as anyone who has a knowledge of church history can easily see. The description is so real that one could almost think that it was written after the development of the Papacy itself.

In this connection the Apostle shows that the seeds of apostasy out of which the Papacy was to grow were already planted, for he says, "The mystery of iniquity doth already work" (vs. 7). Though this church apostate grew up by degrees in the West, it attained great dominion and authority, civil and ecclesiastical, so that Rome became as thoroughly Christian (so-called) as it had previously been pagan. In fact, it was simply the Roman Empire in the West in another form, arrayed in a Christian garb instead of a heathen one. It is, therefore, described in the prophecies of the Revelation as the successor of the dragon, or heathen Rome, reigning in his stead and exercising his dominion and power.

"And I stood upon the sand of the sea, and saw a beast rise up out of the sea, having seven heads and ten horns, and upon his horns ten crowns, and upon his heads the name of blasphemy. And the beast which I saw was like unto a leopard, and his feet were as the feet of a bear, and his mouth as the mouth of a lion: and the dragon gave him his power, and his seat, and great authority" (Rev. 13:1-2).

The heads and horns of this beast prove his substantial identity with the dragon of chapter 12, as already explained. Verse 3 of chapter 13 says that one of his seven heads was wounded, then healed, after which "all the world wondered after the beast" and worshiped him. The explanation is to be found in Revelation 17, where the same beast appears again with its seven heads and ten horns (vs. 3). Here the seven heads are represented as seven kings, or powers—the seven distinct forms of government that ruled successively in the Roman Empire.

These heads and horns, however, pertained to the beast simply as a political power. The ecclesiastical part is in this seventeenth chapter described under the symbol of a corrupt woman sitting on this beast and directing it, which thus describes the Papacy to the very letter. "And I saw a woman sit upon a scarlet-colored beast, full of names of blasphemy, having seven heads and ten horns. And the woman was arrayed in purple and scarlet color, and decked with gold and precious stones and pearls, having a golden cup in her hand full of abominations and filthiness of her fornication: and upon her forehead was a name written, MYSTERY, BABYLON THE GREAT, THE MOTHER OF HARLOTS AND ABOMINATIONS OF THE EARTH. And I saw the woman drunken with the blood of the saints, and with the blood of the martyrs of Jesus: and when I saw her, I wondered with great admiration" (Rev. 17:3-6).

This description agrees with chapter 13, to which I have already referred, where the beast power, *as a beast,* represents the political dominion; while the ecclesiastical, or church, phase is represented by the *human characteristics ascribed to the beast,* one of which is persecution. "And it was given unto him to make war with the saints, and to overcome them: and power was given him over all kindreds, and tongues, and nations" (vs. 7).*

---

*For a comprehensive and detailed description of the Papacy set forth in these prophecies—its substantial identity with heathenism, its extravagant claims, its violent persecutions, the practical universality of its sway, and the time prophecies concerning the length of its undisputed reign, culminating in the great Sixteenth Century Reformation, I refer the reader to my book, *The Revelation Explained,* pp. 128-138, 169-185.

Chapter 18

THE PROTESTANT ERA

The Reformation of the Sixteenth Century broke the power of Rome's spiritual supremacy. Europe was shaken from end to end by a power which it had never known before. The great secret of the early successes of the reformers was their appeal from the decisions of councils and the doctrines and commandments of men to the Word of God itself. And as long as the Word and the Spirit of God were allowed their proper place as the governors of God's people, the power and inspiration of God rested upon the work of the Reformation. This spiritual work of reformation reached its climax about A.D. 1530, the date of the Augsburg Confession. To this date we must point both for the end of Rome's universal spiritual supremacy and for the rise of Protestantism.

Within a few years the followers of the reformers were divided into hostile sects and began to oppose and persecute each other. Luther denounced Zwingli as a heretic, and "the Calvinists would have no dealings with the Lutherans."

The first Protestant creed was the Augsburg Confession, 1530. This date marks an important epoch. From this time the reformation people began to lose sight of the Word and Spirit of God as their governors. They organized themselves into sects, made their own regulations, creeds, and disciplines; and these they upheld by every means possible. From this it will be seen that the rise of Protestantism (organized sectarianism) in 1530 introduced another period of apostasy, or rather another form of the Apostasy, as distinct in many of its features as was that of Romanism before it.

Protestantism in Prophecy

This great system of Protestantism that succeeded Romanism and took first place in the modern religious world was also set forth in the prophecies. The Revelator, after symbolically describing the first beast and its reign, continues:

"And I beheld another beast coming up out of the earth; and he had two horns like a lamb, and he spake as a dragon. And he exerciseth all the power of the first beast before him, and causeth the earth and them which dwell therein to worship the first beast, whose deadly wound was healed (Rev. 13:11-12).

It is certainly consistent with the divine plan that Protestantism should be portrayed in prophecy. From the time the religion of God became definitely associated with successive world empires and political dominion, beginning with the Babylonian Empire, there has been a corresponding and continuous prophetic outline of God's unfolding work in the world.

In this description by the Revelator, however, the special actions ascribed to this beast—speaking, working miracles, deceiving, making an image, imparting life to it, all of which belong properly to the department of human life—show conclusively that it is the character of this beast as an *ecclesiastical* power that is the chief point under consideration. He had political power, it is true, though he was not to become such a terrible beast politically (for his horns were only like a lamb), but "he spake as a dragon." As soon as we enter the department to which "speaking" by analogy refers us, we find this beast to be a great religious power; and it is in this character alone that he is delineated in the remaining verses of the chapter. That the description of a religious system is the main burden of this symbol is also shown by the fact that this beast is in every case in subsequent chapters of the Revelation referred to as the "false prophet" (16:13; 19:20; 20:10).

The Image of the Beast

This second beast, or Protestantism as a religion, was to make an image of the first beast. "Image" is defined to be "an imitation, representation, or similitude of any person or thing; a copy, a likeness, an effigy." The second beast, then, is to manufacture something in *imitation* of the first beast. But which phase of the first beast, political or ecclesiastical, is to be copied? "The image of the beast should . . . *speak*." This directs us by analogy to religious affairs; therefore, the copy is a human *ecclesiastical organization* in imitation of the hierarchy of Rome.

The Roman Church is a humanly organized institution, governed, like the kingdom of the world, by an authority centralized in a self-perpetuating human headship. Protestant sects likewise are human organizations, each being governed by a man or a conference of men. The Roman Catholic Church makes and prescribes the theology that her members believe. Protestant churches also make their own disciplines and prescribe rules of faith and practice. Such a system is foreign to the original conception of the church as embracing the whole spiritual brotherhood under the moral and spiritual dominion of Christ. It is contrary to the plain teachings of the Bible, which condemn divisions and enjoin unity and oneness upon the redeemed of the Lord.

We freely acknowledge that during the Protestant Era there have been great reformations in which God worked mightily in the salvation of men and women and from which great good has accrued to the race. But looking back from the present point of view, we can see that these reformations were only partial. They did not restore all the primitive truth of Christianity. In fact, when these various movements became thoroughly established and widely known, their people, made confident of God's approval through past successes, were thereby deceived into taking another step—*making an image*—and organizing themselves into ecclesiastical bodies with their own disciplines and rules.

It is evident that such an exhibition of churchianity is not a consistent portrayal of pure apostolic Christianity as experienced in primitive days and as recorded in, and required by, the Scriptures of God.*

---

*For an extended discussion of Protestantism in prophecy, its fundamental character, the "name of the beast," the "mark of the beast," the "number of his name," Protestantism as a persecuting power, the period of Protestant expansion and reign, and other subjects, I urge the reader to consult my book, *The Revelation Explained*, pp. 186-197.

Chapter 19

THE TRUE CHURCH RESTORED

In the two preceding chapters we have briefly considered the first and second beasts of Revelation 13, showing that they symbolize two great systems of religion—Roman Catholicism and Protestantism. The same twofold form of the Apostasy is also described in other parts of the Revelation under the general term "Babylon," as we shall now show; and in this connection a final restoration is also predicted.

A Restoration Predicted

In Revelation 17, to which reference has already been made, a beast with seven heads and ten horns is brought to view, agreeing with the first beast of chapter 13. Here (chap. 17) the beast is the Western Roman Empire under the papal form, with the papal church symbolized by a corrupt woman seated upon this beast and directing its course. Outwardly, the richly adorned woman presented a splendid appearance, but her true character was symbolized by the contents of the golden cup she held in her hand, it being "full of abominations and filthiness of her fornication: and upon her forehead was a name written, MYSTERY, BABYLON THE GREAT, THE MOTHER OF HARLOTS AND ABOMINATIONS OF THE EARTH" (vss. 3-5).

The remaining verses of the chapter describe the manner in which the beast would support the woman for ages, after which the ten horns (or minor kingdoms) would turn against her and "make her desolate and naked, and shall eat her flesh, and burn her with fire. For God hath put in their hearts to fulfill his will, and to agree, and give their kingdom unto the beast, until the words of God shall be fulfilled" (vss. 16-17). That Rome possessed and exercised temporal power during many centuries all historians know. The last part of this prediction was fulfilled when King Victor Emmanuel entered Rome in 1870 and established the free government of United

129

Italy, at which time the pope's temporal sovereignty, vested in the Papal States from the time of Pepin and Charlemagne, was abolished. So 1870 marks the time when the woman was indeed made "desolate and naked," the time when "the words of God shall be fulfilled."

"And after these things I saw another angel come down from heaven, having great power; and the earth was lightened with his glory. And he cried mightily with a strong voice, saying, Babylon the great is fallen, is fallen, and is become the habitation of devils, and the hold of every foul spirit, and a cage of every unclean and hateful bird. For all nations have drunk of the wine of the wrath of her fornication. . . . And I heard another voice from heaven, saying, Come out of her, my people, that ye be not partakers of her sins, and that ye receive not of her plagues" (Rev. 18:1-4).

A spiritual movement of mighty power is symbolized in these verses, and as it was to take place *after* the fulfillment of the things described in chapter 17, it could not take place before the year 1870, when the temporal power of the pope ceased. This movement calls forth the people of God from spiritual Babylon, which is "fallen."

What Babylon Includes

Protestants often limit "Babylon the Great" to the Church of Rome, because the woman symbolizing the apostate church (chap. 17) is denominated "Babylon the Great" (vs. 5). But the same verse also declares her to be the "mother of harlots," and if she, a degraded woman, stands as the representative of a corrupt church her unchaste daughters must at least symbolize churches that are her descendants. If the real name of the mother is Babylon, as stated, the proper name of her harlot daughters must be Babylon also. Whether, therefore, the mother or the daughters are mentioned in a given instance, the reference is to "Babylon," because it is all the same family, connected with the "great city which reigneth over the kings of the earth" (vs. 18).

The term "Babylon" has even a more extensive application than Papacy and Protestantism. It doubtless includes the whole city of sect confusion, the babel of all man-made institutions called churches.

Admitted by Protestants

That the term "Babylon" includes Protestantism and also that the fallen condition ascribed to her is in accordance with the facts, may be abundantly proved by the testimonies of leading Protestants themselves.*

Testimony of the Word

Let us appeal to the prophecies to show definitely that this heavenly cry against Babylon really includes Protestantism also.

Returning to Revelation 13, we again observe that Catholicism is symbolized by the first beast, and Protestantism by the second beast, whose man-made religious forms and institutions constitute an *image* to the first beast. Therefore, we have in that chapter the twofold form of the Apostasy—papal and Protestant. Immediately following (chap. 14) we have a strikingly contrasted description of the true people of God. They are following the Lamb, not wandering after the beast. They are marked by having their "Father's name in their foreheads," not with the mark and name of the beast. They are worshiping Christ and giving glory to him, not bowing down before the beast or his image. The whole Word of God did not have free course under the reign of the second beast, but we have here (14:6-7) clearly predicted a *final restoration* message and movement in which the whole truth is presented to the world.

Babylon Is Fallen

The restoration of the pure gospel after the reign of the two beasts is thus clearly predicted. But this is not all of the message; for the same light that reveals the pure word of Heaven's truth reveals also the fallen condition of Babylon. "And there followed another angel, saying, Babylon is fallen, is fallen, that great city, because she made all nations drink of the wine of the wrath of her fornication. And the third angel followed them, saying with a loud voice, If any man worship the beast

*For specific quotations, see pp. 238-240 of the unabridged edition.

and his image, and receive his mark in his forehead, or in his hand, the same shall drink of the wine of the wrath of God, which is poured out without mixture into the cup of his indignation" (Rev. 14:8-10).

Here we find that the heavenly message against Babylon, "that great city," is directed against both the beast *and his image*. Now, the "image" was made by the second beast, or Protestantism (13:14); therefore, the command to come out of Babylon applies to those who are in Protestantism. In other words, it applies to the whole unscriptural system of man-made and man-controlled organizations called churches.

God's People Called Out

Notice, also, that the message of the two angels of chapter 14 is the same, and in the same order, as those in Revelation 18:1-4, already noticed. The first one cries, "Babylon is fallen, is fallen" (14:8). The next one warns the people against worshiping the beast or his image, upon the terrible penalty of receiving the wrath of God. So also in chapter 18 the first angel cries, "Babylon the great is fallen, is fallen" (vs. 2). Then is heard, "another voice from heaven, saying, Come out of her, my people, that ye be not partakers of her sins, and that ye receive not of her plagues" (vs. 4).

While the woman, or pure church, in the morning of this dispensation was driven "into the wilderness," we thank God that she was not always to remain there; and in this final restoration movement, or reformation, she is to come forth out of the great wilderness of the Apostasy and, as the bride of Christ, return to Zion. "Who is this that cometh up from the wilderness, leaning upon her beloved?" (Song of Sol. 8:5). "Who is she that looketh forth as the morning, fair as the moon, clear as the sun, and terrible as an army with banners?" (6:10). It is the true church of God.

The prophecies that describe this final restoration are not confined to the Revelation. They may be found even in the Old Testament.

The gospel as preached by the Apostles out of the Sacred Writings was from the Old Testament—the only Scriptures they had then. Peter says that Old Testament "prophets have inquired and searched diligently, who prophesied of the grace that should come unto you . . . the sufferings of Christ, and the glory that should follow. Unto whom it was revealed, that not unto themselves, but unto us they did minister the things, which are now reported unto you by them that have preached the gospel unto you with the Holy Ghost sent down from heaven" (I Pet. 1:10-12).

According to the Apostles, the chief object of Old Testament prophecy was *the gospel age,* with its glories *to follow* the sufferings of Christ. Therefore they stated, over and over again, "It came to pass that it might be fulfilled which was spoken by the prophet." The entire Book of Hebrews shows that the special design of God in the typology of the Old Testament was to set forth the house of God, the true New Testament church of God, "whose house are we." So the church is the subject and object of Old Testament typology and prophecy.

Again I say, the prophecies that describe the final restoration of God's true church are not confined to the Revelation. Zechariah clearly predicts it thus [I will give this verse as rendered in the *Septuagint Version,* for it is clearer there]: "And it shall come to pass in that day [the papal day] that there shall be no light, and there shall be for one day [the Protestant day] cold and frost, and that day shall be known to the Lord, it shall not be day nor night [a mixture of light and darkness]: but towards evening it shall be light" (Zech. 14:6-7). Thank God for the light of the evening time!

This same spiritual movement is predicted by Ezekiel, who describes the people of God under the figure of sheep: "And ye my flock, the flock of my pasture, are men" (34:31). These sheep of the Lord are represented as oppressed, driven away, abused, and scattered by false shepherds, or preachers. God says, "My sheep wandered through all the mountains, and upon every high hill [from one sect to another]: yea, my flock was scattered upon all the face of the earth" (vs. 6).

Read carefully the whole chapter. It is a prophetic, true-to-fact picture of the experiences of God's people scattered during the dark and cloudy day of Protestantism. But the work of final reformation is predicted in verses 11-12: "For thus saith the Lord God; Behold I, even I, will both search my sheep, and seek them out. As a shepherd seeketh out his flock in the day that he is among his sheep that are scattered; so will I seek out my sheep, and will deliver them out of all places where they have been scattered in the cloudy and dark day."

When the Apostles apply obscure Old Testament texts to conditions and events in the gospel age, we accept their application on the ground of apostolic authority. Now let it be remembered that our application of Zion, Jerusalem, Babylon, and other terms, to conditions and events in the latter part of this present age is no mere analogical reasoning of ours: it is the inspired Apostle John himself who thus applies these things in the Revelation. We accept the analogies, the applications, the true-to-fact symbolisms as divine inspiration.

Babylon is fallen, the divine record states, and God is said to be calling his people out. To stay there, yoked up with multitudes of godless and graceless professors of religion, who are lovers of this world, means finally to lose spiritual life. The Apostle Paul utters words which contain a principle applicable in this case: "Be ye not unequally yoked together with unbelievers; for what fellowship hath righteousness with unrighteousness? and what communion hath light with darkness? . . . Wherefore come out from among them, and be ye separate, saith the Lord, and touch not the unclean thing; and I will receive you, and will be a Father unto you, and ye shall be my sons and daughters, saith the Lord Almighty" (II Cor. 6:14, 17-18).

They Are Called to Zion

When the people of God hear this heavenly message to come out of Babylon, and they obey, where shall they go? Shall they wander around, independent of each other, over the spiritual deserts of the earth? No! Let the Word of God settle this point. The experiences of natural Israel under the Old Testament dispensation foreshadow, and thus describe, in many respects the experiences of God's spiritual Israel, or church, in the New Testament dispensation. The Revelator himself draws these analogies, thus giving them apostolic and authoritative sanction. As Israel was led captive to literal Babylon, so the church has been held captive in spiritual Babylon. As literal

Babylon was overthrown, and the Jews made their escape, so spiritual Babylon "is fallen, is fallen," and God's people are commanded to "come out of her."

What did literal Israel do when they came out of Babylon? They made their way *in a body* direct to Mount Zion, where formerly the temple of Jehovah stood in magnificent glory, and began at once the work of restoration under the direction and the approval of God. And the work at Jerusalem prospered, because "the people had a mind to work" (Neh. 4:6). Thus shall it be with those who make their escape from spiritual Babylon: "The ransomed of the Lord shall return, and come to Zion with songs and everlasting joy upon their heads: they shall obtain joy and gladness, and sorrow and sighing shall flee away" (Isa. 35:10). The purpose of such a movement is the restoration of a pure church, or temple of God, as in apostolic days—a church dedicated by the Holy Spirit and filled with the power and glory of God. "He that is not with me is against me; and he that gathereth not with me scattereth abroad" (Matt. 12:30).

Restoration a Necessity

A final restoration of the true church of God before the end of time is not only desirable but necessary. Such a movement is not dependent on prophecy, nor on anyone's particular interpretation of prophecy; it is made necessary and inevitable because of the nature of the church itself.

Sectarianism, however, is not altogether modern. In fact, the original church itself was built wholly out of sectarians. In those days everybody was religious, identified with some party or group. The Jews themselves were broken up into a number of rival sects and parties, such as "the sect of the Pharisees" (Acts 15:5)—"the most straitest sect of our religion," Paul said (26:5)—and Sadducees, Essenes, and Herodians. The entire Gentile world consisted of religious groups and parties of all kinds.

Into such a confused and hopelessly divided religious world Christ came and built his church. How did he do it? Was it done by accepting or joining any one of those sects? Was it by recognition of the existing religious condition? Was it by an organic confederation of them all, or by a broad, tolerant, intermingling process? Not at all. Good people there were in all these sects, of course, but they had been misled, blinded, deceived. Saul of Tarsus was one of that kind, but when God finished with him on that Damascus highway and in the house of Judas, all sectarianism was entirely gone from him. By a divine process he and all other honest and God-fearing people were separated from sects and sectarianism, were reconciled "unto God in one body by the cross" (Eph. 2:16), "called in one body" (Col. 3:15), united "for his body's sake, which is the church" (1:24). Thus the apostolic church was built out of the good material already existing in that old-time sectarianism. But it was done by spiritual processes, by the mighty power of the Spirit of God. And since God accomplished this miracle once, it is but reasonable to suppose that he both can and will do it again.

There is no way to square organized denominationalism with the Word of God—with the one divinely organized church of God, as set in order and ruled by the one Spirit of God. The only way under heaven to realize and to exhibit in practice again the visible unity of believers for which Christ prayed in John 17 is to *forsake all the doctrines, commandments, and sectarian divisions of men* and to abide in Christ alone.

According to the prophecies, there will be a final church restoration before the end of time. It is represented as being accomplished by God calling his people out of, *and outside of,* Babylon, thus preparing the bride for the coming of the Bridegroom. (See again Rev. 18—19.) Such a movement is not—and cannot be—a geographically defined and limited colonization scheme, but, like the primitive church itself, it must be a great spiritual state and ideal whose true center of gravity is Christ himself in all his revealed truth. Whenever and wherever people of God accept the Christ in the fullness of his divine power, in his complete rule as active and actual head of the church—wherever the Holy Spirit is not only permitted to take full possession of individual hearts, but also to have absolute spiritual dominion over the collective assembly of the saints, thus destroying every principle of sectarian divisions and effectually breaking down denominational walls separating God's people—then, no matter what the geographical location, the physical barriers, or the natural separations such as language differences, *then and there* is a concrete exhibition of the restored church of God.

So far as we can see, no prophetic time limitations are placed on this final church restoration period. Whether it will be one century or five centuries nobody knows. The work must be done, and time is not particularly important; the fact that there is to be such a restoration is the really important thing.

To us who live in these last days it is inspiring to know that this work of restoration has already begun.* Countless thousands, awakening to the unscripturalness of sectarianism, and discerning by the Spirit "the body of Christ," which alone is the church, have forsaken that which is only human in order to abide in, and represent properly and scripturally, the body of Christ, the true church of the living God. This work is also being attested and confirmed by the manifestation of his glorious power. Men who are possessed with devils, men whose cases are as bad as those described in the New Testament—the victims lying on the floor, writhing under demon influence, foaming and frothing at the mouth, and uttering horrible cries —are delivered by the power of God, restored to their right minds, and made to worship and praise God. God is indeed "confirming the word with signs following" (Mark 16:20). The eyes of the blind are opened, the ears of the deaf unstopped, the lame made to leap as an hart, and the tongue of the dumb to sing. Cancer and tuberculosis, rheumatism and heart trouble, appendicitis and nervous prostration, and other diseases of almost every description and name are, in hundreds and thousands of instances, healed by divine power. I myself have witnessed the healing of thousands.

Triumphant over the Apostasy

To witness such results, after the long reign of the beast and his image, is enough to start songs of rejoicing among the angels of heaven and to awaken shouts and praises among the redeemed of earth. When the Israelites were in Babylonian

*For a fuller treatment of this subject, see my specialized works, *Prophetic Lectures on Daniel and the Revelation* (now out of print but available in some church libraries) and *The Revelation Explained.*

bondage, sadly they hung their harps upon the willows by the riverside and wept when they "remembered Zion." Here they were tormented by their captors, who said, "Sing us one of the songs of Zion"; and they answered, despairingly, "How shall we sing the Lord's song in a strange land?" (Ps. 137:1-4). Zion's songs were *songs of deliverance;* therefore it was not possible to sing them in a strange land.

So has it been in spiritual Babylon. The truly saved held captive therein during the long reign of apostasy have had their righteous souls vexed from day to day with the pride, the worldliness, and the ungodliness of their surroundings; and there they have wept and groaned when they remembered Zion's primitive condition. At the same time, however, they have been expected to be happy and to sing the songs of Zion. How could they sing these songs of deliverance in a strange land? Impossible! It is when "the ransomed of the Lord return, and come to Zion," that the "songs and everlasting joy" break forth again. And this was described by the Revelator: "And I saw as it were a sea of glass mingled with fire: and them that had gotten the victory over the beast, and over his image, and over his mark, and over the number of his name, stand on the sea of glass having the harps of God. And they sing the song of Moses the servant of God [a song of deliverance], and the song of the Lamb [a song of redemption], saying, Great and marvelous are thy works, Lord God Almighty; just and true are thy ways, thou King of saints" (Rev. 15:2-3). Thank God! Since we have returned from Babylon we have our harps once more and are able to sing the songs of Zion. Hallelujah!

CONCERNING DIVINE LAW AND THE KINGDOM OF GOD

Chapter 20

THE TWO COVENANTS

In Galatians 4:21-31 two covenants are brought to view. The first proceeds from Sinai and "gendereth to bondage"; the second is associated with "Jerusalem which is above . . . the mother of us all." They therefore represent the two great systems by which God has governed his people on earth: first, by the Law system, which originated at Sinai; second, by the gospel, which came through Christ.

These two covenants are represented by the Apostle as the mothers of God's people, prefigured by the two wives of Abraham. Hagar, the bondmaid, represents the Law system, and her son, Ishmael, signifies the Jewish nation, the "children" of that covenant; Sarah, the free wife, represents the gospel system, and Isaac, her son, signifies all true believers in Christ, who are "children," not "of the bondwoman, but of the free." These systems are not to continue side by side, but the one is the successor of the other in the Father's favor—the Law system, with all its "children" (Hagar and Ishmael), being rejected for the true gospel system (Sarah and Isaac). "Cast out the bondwoman and her son: for the son of the bondwoman shall not be heir with the son of the freewoman." We of the gospel dispensation "as Isaac was, are the children of promise."

The Meaning of the Covenant

A study of the Bible use of the term "covenant," meaning a contract between God and man, shows that it signifies God's promise of unmerited favors and blessings to man, generally through *some particular system* by which they are to be enjoyed. For this reason his "covenant" is used interchangeably with his "counsel," "oath," or "promise."

The covenant which "he made with Abraham, and his oath unto Isaac," promised to give the land of Canaan to the Jews. The entire Abrahamic covenant is thus regarded simply as a divine *promise,* and not in any sense a mutual agreement. (For proof see Heb. 6:13-15; Gal. 3:14-18; Luke 1:68-75.)

The promise of a coming Redeemer is termed "God's covenant"; yet who would think of suggesting that such was the result of a mutual contract, or obligation, made between God and man? It is a covenant indeed, yet it is all one-sided and consists of God's gratuitous blessing. (See Isa. 59:20-21.)

We have already shown that God has made two special covenants, each of which embraces an entire system of divine law and government in a distinct dispensation of time. These we desire especially to set forth, showing their establishment, nature, duration, and special relations to each other.

The Sinaitic Covenant

The first covenant, the one afterwards "cast out," came, we are told, "from the mount Sinai"; therefore, we shall consult the Bible in order to see what constitutes that covenant from Sinai.

The Decalogue, or Ten Commandments. "And he was there [in Mount Sinai] . . . forty days and forty nights; he did neither eat bread, nor drink water. And he wrote upon the tables the words of the covenant, the ten commandments" (Exod. 34:28). "And he declared unto you his covenant, which he commanded you to perform, even ten commandments; and he wrote them upon two tables of stone" (Deut. 4:13).

These two passages declare positively that the Ten Commandments, written on tables of stone, constituted the Sinaitic covenant. This fact is even more clearly stated, if possible, in Deuteronomy 5:2-22.

Other precepts also. But while the Decalogue, as the foregoing Scripture texts show, constituted the covenant proper, other precepts given on Sinai were included in that covenant. "I made a covenant with your fathers in the day that I brought them forth out of the land of Egypt, out of the house of bondmen, saying, At the end of seven years let ye go every man his brother an Hebrew, which hath been sold unto thee" (Jer.

34:13-14). This last-named precept is from Exodus 21:2, and was therefore contained in the book of the covenant that Moses wrote just after God first spoke on Sinai. At that time God gave the Ten Commandments, together with certain other laws, statutes, judgments, and ordinances; whereupon "Moses wrote all the words of the Lord" (which included the Decalogue) in a little book containing what is now Exodus 20—23. Here "covenant" is expanded to include the little book, for the simple reason that the book contained the covenant proper —the Ten Commandments. Had they not been included in this writing of Moses, we might know little concerning them, because the stone tables upon which they were written have disappeared.

The entire Pentateuch. At a later time Moses wrote a large book, the Pentateuch, comprising what is now the first five books of the Bible, and in this he included the little book just mentioned. Now, since "the book of the covenant," which had been dedicated by blood, was incorporated in the complete writings of Moses, the entire work became known as "the book of the covenant," embracing the whole Mosaic, or Law, system—moral, civil, and ceremonial. Paul regards the old covenant as identical with the writings of Moses—the Pentateuch (II Cor. 3:14-15, RSV). Now, this is the broadest use of the term "covenant" that we have in the Bible. This book of the Law is termed "the covenant" because it contains, is built upon, and centers in the covenant proper—the Ten Commandments. (See Exod. 34:28 and Deut. 4:13; 5:2-22).

The foregoing Scripture texts show positively that the covenant from Sinai was one, and that it included the Decalogue and all other precepts and commandments, whether civil, moral, or ceremonial.

A New Covenant Predicted

"Behold, the days come, saith the Lord, that I will make a new covenant with the house of Israel, and with the house of Judah: not according to the covenant that I made with their fathers in the day that I took them by the hand to bring them out of the land of Egypt; which my covenant they break, although I was an husband unto them, saith the Lord: but this shall be the covenant that I will make with the house of Israel; After those days, saith the Lord, I will put my law in their inward parts, and write it in their hearts; and will be their God, and they shall be my people. And they shall teach no more every man his neighbor, and every man his brother, saying, Know the Lord: for they shall all know me, from the least of them unto the greatest of them, saith the Lord: for I will forgive their iniquity, and I will remember their sin no more" (Jer. 31:31-34).

This new covenant was established by Jesus Christ: "By so much was Jesus made a surety of a better testament" (Heb. 7:22). "But now hath he obtained a more excellent ministry; by how much also he is the mediator of a better covenant, which was established upon better promises" (8:6). In every respect this new covenant through Christ is better than the old one.

1. It *"was established upon better promises."* The Mosaic covenant was based upon those promises in the original Abrahamic covenant which pertain to the literal Israel, hence was limited—national; whereas, the "better covenant" is based upon those promises in the Abrahamic covenant which have universal import, meeting their fulfillment in the gospel of Jesus Christ.

2. It *has a better mediator.* "The law was given by Moses" (John 1:17), whereas Jesus is "the mediator of the new covenant" (Heb. 12:24; 8:6).

3. It *has a better priesthood.* The priests of the Law were fallible men, who "were not suffered to continue by reason of death" (Heb. 7:23), whereas Jesus is our high priest, and he is "holy, harmless, undefiled, separate from sinners, and made higher than the heavens," and "because he continueth ever, hath an unchangeable priesthood" (7:26, 24).

4. It *has a better sanctuary.* "The first covenant had . . . a worldly sanctuary" (Heb. 9:1). The new covenant sanctuary, temple, or house of God is his spiritual church (I Pet. 2:5; Heb. 3:6; I Tim. 3:15; Eph. 2:19-22).

5. It *has a better sacrifice.* Instead of the "blood of bulls and of goats," "which can never take away sins" (Heb. 9:13; 10:11), the new covenant was sealed with "the blood of Christ,"

which is able to "purge your conscience from dead works to serve the living God" (9:14).

The First Covenant Abolished

Throughout the Book of Hebrews these two covenants are placed in sharp contrast, and the first covenant is declared to have been abolished.

The weakness of the old covenant was one of the causes of its abolition. "For there is verily a disannulling of the commandment going before for the weakness and unprofitableness thereof. For the law made nothing perfect, but the bringing in of a better hope did; by the which we draw nigh unto God. . . . By so much was Jesus made a surety of a better testament" (Heb. 7:18-19, 22). In the new covenant there is perfect salvation from sin through the blood of Jesus Christ.

The abolition of the first covenant and the establishment of the second covenant is set forth in Hebrews 8:6-13 in the plainest manner.

These two covenants are also contrasted by Paul in II Corinthians 3:3-14. Here the first covenant is described as the "old testament," "tables of stone," "the ministration of death," which "was glorious" at that time, the "letter" which "killeth," "the ministration of condemnation," and that which was "written and engraven in stones," which was "done away" and "abolished." The second covenant is the "new testament," of which Paul was an able minister; "the Spirit," which "giveth life"; "the ministration of the Spirit"; "the glory that excelleth"; that which "remaineth" and is "written in the fleshly tables of the heart."

Chapter 21

"THE LAW OF CHRIST"

As we showed in the preceding chapter, the national law of
the Israelites enacted on Mount Sinai constituted the first, or
old, covenant and was abolished by Christ at the cross; that is,
so far as God's sanction and approval were concerned, the
Mosaic law ended then, for it had served its temporary purpose
as a standard of duty and judgment among God's people. It
was only "added because of transgressions, till the seed should
come to whom the [Abrahamic] promise was made," "which is
Christ" (Gal. 3:19, 16).

The Necessity of Law

There still exists, however, the necessity of law as a standard
of judgment, because without law there could be no sin, "for
sin is the transgression of the law" (I John 3:4). Therefore,
without a law defining and limiting human actions and conduct
there could be no sin, hence no pardon or salvation.

Now our moral obligations, our conduct and actions, are of
a twofold character, embracing the relationship we hold to
our fellow men and also the relationship we hold to God whose
creatures and subjects we are. For this reason, a perfect law,
covering all human conduct and defining sin, *must proceed
from God.*

Only Divine Law Can Define Sin

Since a law capable of defining sin must proceed from God,
and since, as we have shown, the Mosaic system has been
abolished by Christ, what law now furnishes the standard of
judgment for the world? Under what law are Christians?

"God, who at sundry times and in divers manners spake in
time past unto the fathers by the prophets, hath in these last
days spoken unto us by his Son" (Heb. 1:1-2). God's requirements can be made known to men only by revelation, and this
he made known "unto the fathers by the prophets" in various

144

ways and at different times. Do not overlook this fact; it is important. As we showed in a preceding chapter, divine revelation was by necessity a gradual, progressive process, in accommodation to human conditions. For this reason, commandments and obligations that God has laid upon men in one period of time have often been superseded, in the order of God's plan, by something of a higher and more perfect nature. If men fail to understand this principle, they may, like the Israelites of old, attempt to perpetuate some of God's appointments long after he himself is done with them.

Christ the Lawgiver

Now, when God speaks to men, is not his word law? Is it right to disobey? And if his word is law, then there can be no higher law than "the law of Christ"; for Jesus himself says, "I and my Father are one" (John 10:30). He asserts that "all men should honor the Son, even as they honor the Father" (5:23). So far as authority is concerned, then, Christ is supreme. If he delivered a law, that law must be final, must be binding upon all, and must be the standard of judgment for the world. God "hath . . . spoken unto us by his Son."

In the Old Testament we have clear predictions of the coming of another lawgiver. Moses himself, the mediator of the old law, understood that his system was to be temporary and prophesied of a change (Deut. 18:15, 17-19). This passage teaches that God's words which this prophet should speak would be the standard of judgment for the disobedient—"I will require it of him." In Acts 3:22-23, Peter quotes this prophecy and applies it directly to Jesus Christ, whose word is law—"the law of Christ." Isaiah, with clear reference to Christ, says, "The isles shall wait for his law" (42:4). "His law," "the law of Christ," was not in existence in Isaiah's day, but men were obliged to "wait" for it. After the lapse of many centuries it came, thank God!

Follow this divine Lawgiver to the Mount of Transfiguration. Here appear Moses and Elias—Moses representing the Law that he delivered and the dispensation that he ushered in; Elias, the foremost man among all the prophets of the old dispensation, representing all the prophets through whom "God spake in time past unto the fathers." Peter, amazed by the supernatural illumination of his Lord and overawed with the splendor of the occasion, said, "Lord, it is good for us to be here: if thou wilt, let us make here three tabernacles: one for thee, and one for Moses, and one for Elias" (Matt. 17:4). Peter seemed to think that all three should be accorded equal honor and place in the worship of God. Listen to the rebuke of Heaven at the very suggestion: "While he yet spake, behold, a bright cloud overshadowed them: and behold a voice out of the cloud, which said, This is my beloved Son, in whom I am well pleased; hear ye him. . . . And when they had lifted up their eyes, they saw no man, save Jesus only" (vss. 5, 8).

Neither Moses and the Law, nor Elias, nor the other prophets can stand with Him who claims equality with God— "Jesus only." The first covenant was revealed on Mount Sinai and amid great manifestations; how appropriate, then, that the actual change to the new covenant should be made known on a mountain in this marvelous manner, with the seal and approval of Heaven itself upon the demonstration! "The law was given by Moses, but grace and truth came by Jesus Christ" (John 1:17). "The law and the prophets were until John [who baptized Christ]: since that time the kingdom of God is preached" (Luke 16:16). In the order of his plan, God "spake in time past unto the fathers by the prophets," but now he "hath in these last days spoken unto us by his Son." O children of earth, know ye that God hath spoken unto us by his Son. "Hear ye him!"

The New Law God's Standard of Judgment

According to the prediction of Moses, God promised to place his words in the mouth of the new prophet, or lawgiver. In fulfillment of this, Jesus says: "I have not spoken of myself; but the Father which sent me, he gave me a commandment, what I should say, and what I should speak. And I know that his commandment is life everlasting: whatsoever I speak therefore, even as the Father said unto me, so I speak" (John 12:49-50).

This law of commandments delivered by Christ defines sin and is the present standard of judgment. This is proved by the fact that it is the standard by which we shall be judged in the last great day (vs. 48). Our responsibility is now rated, not by the Decalogue, nor the Law of Moses, nor the injunctions of the prophets, but by the "gospel," the law of Christ.

1. *Christ possessed all authority.* "All power is given unto me in heaven and in earth" (Matt. 28:18).

2. *He taught with authority.* "He taught them as one having authority" (Matt. 7:29). His teachings throughout show a directness characteristic of an original lawgiver. Not once does he quote law or prophet as *his authority* for his teaching. He quotes them for other purposes, but for his doctrine he claims no authority besides God.

Some people affirm that in Matthew 5 Christ is simply enlarging the scope of the old law; but notice that a series of striking contrasts are here introduced. He refers to the Law in the words, "Ye have heard that it hath been said"; whereas he introduces his own teaching thus: "But I say unto you." His standard is not the Law standard, but another standard, and a higher one, and it proceeds directly from him.

In introducing this higher law Christ paid his respects to the old law and the prophets that had prepared the way for him—"Think not that I am come to destroy the law, or the prophets: I am not come to destroy, but to fulfill. For verily I say unto you, Till heaven and earth pass, one jot or one tittle shall in no wise pass from the law, till all be fulfilled" (Matt. 5:17-18).

3. *Christ delivered a law.* "The law of Christ" (Gal. 6:2).

4. *It is binding on Christians.* "Go ye therefore, and teach all nations . . . teaching them to observe [the law?—No! but] all things whatsoever I have commanded you" (Matt. 28:19-20). Now, these "commandments" of Christ constitute the message to all nations. Mark states it thus: "And he said unto them, Go ye into all the world, and preach the gospel to every creature" (Mark 16:15). The gospel, then, contains the commandments of God binding on Christians, and they were delivered by Christ. For this reason Paul acknowledged himself as being "under the law of Christ" (I Cor. 9:21)—"under the law of the Messiah" (Syriac Version).

5. *We must keep these commandments.* "If ye love me,

keep my commandments" (John 14:15). "If a man love me, he will keep my words" (vs. 23). "Ye are my friends, if ye do whatsoever I command you. . . . For all things that I have heard of my Father I have made known unto you" (15:14-15). Some imagine that by observing the Decalogue they are keeping the commandments of God. Not so. The commandments of God in the Christian dispensation are quite another thing, being, as we have shown, the "words," the "commandments," yea, "the gospel," of Jesus Christ; and *by it* we shall be judged in the last day (12:48). This "law of Christ" contains many commandments that are entirely "new," belonging exclusively to this dispensation, such as those pertaining to baptism, the Lord's Supper, and foot washing.

In obedience to the divine commission the Apostles delivered this law to the Christian churches. Paul, who was God's apostle in a special sense (Gal. 1:1), wrote to the Corinthians: "I have received of the Lord that which also I delivered unto you" (I Cor. 11:23). And again, "If any man think himself to be a prophet, or spiritual, let him acknowledge that the things that I write unto you are the commandments of the Lord" (14:37). To the Thessalonians he said, "Ye know what commandments we gave you by the Lord Jesus" (I Thess. 4:2); and he commended them because they had received his preaching, "not as the word of men, but as it is in truth, the word of God" (2:13).

A "Perfect Law of Liberty"

As we have seen, "the law of Christ" is the standard of judgment. In order to be a perfect law defining sin and covering the entire range of human responsibility, it must prohibit everything that is in its nature wrong and enjoin everything that is right.

The gospel standard is the only perfect one. It alone condemns all that is wrong and enjoins all that is right. *It alone is in force.* As the "second" covenant, or "will," it has now superseded in every respect the "first" covenant and is the standard of judgment now, and by it we shall be judged in the last day.

Chapter 22

THE LAW OF HOLINESS

The law of Christ and the two covenants have thus far been considered from the objective standpoint only; that is, as revelations made to man. So far as the old covenant is concerned, this is sufficient. Its laws were simply written in a book, and this writing by Moses was sealed and confirmed to Israel by the two "tables of testimony" on which God himself wrote that part of the Law that all Israel heard him speak. But the new covenant, embodied in our New Testament, is more than an external revelation; it is a "better covenant."

Jeremiah was the first inspired writer who distinctly mentioned the new covenant, and this he placed in sharp contrast with the Mosaic covenant. (See Jer. 31:31-34.)

According to Hebrews 8:8-13 where this prophecy is quoted, Christ established this new covenant. This new covenant is not the Decalogue. It consists of moral laws; for only moral laws can be inscribed in the heart, producing moral revolution in human character.

Originally, this perfect law was written in man's heart—inscribed in his very nature. This original law constituted the moral image of God in man, but it became largely effaced from the human heart as a result of the Fall, so that men, far from God, do not "know" him in that intimate relationship that existed in Eden. In the "new covenant," however, all this is restored.

In perfect salvation the laws of God are written in our hearts. The writer to the Hebrews quotes the prediction of Jeremiah concerning this writing and applies its fulfillment thus: "He hath perfected forever them that are sanctified. Whereof the Holy Ghost also is a witness to us" (10:14-15). Under the old covenant the laws of God were placed in the second, or inner, room of the tabernacle; under the new covenant they are placed in our hearts. In the holy of holies of the tabernacle all the laws of God were placed—written in a book,

149

and sealed and confirmed by the divine "tables of testimony." Likewise, in entire sanctification, in addition to the perfect writing of God's laws in our hearts, "the Holy Ghost also is a witness to us." Our Decalogue now is the Holy Ghost—the exclusive work of God.

Paul says that we "have put on the new man, which is renewed in knowledge after the image of him that created him" (Col. 3:10). "And that ye put on the new man, which after God is created in righteousness and true holiness" (Eph. 4:24). This work is completed in us in entire sanctification, the perfecting grace of God, and is therefore identical with the restoration of God's law in the soul (Heb. 10:14-17).

Let us define more particularly this original, universal, moral law. Since in its restoration it is identified with "righteousness and true holiness" in the wholly sanctified, or perfected, soul, evidently in the Edenic state it was comprehended in man's perfect moral nature. Now what was it?

Jesus gives us an analysis of this subject in the following conversation: "Then one of them, which was a lawyer, asked him a question, tempting him, and saying, Master, which is the great commandment in the law? Jesus said unto him, Thou shalt love the Lord thy God with all thy heart, and with all thy soul, and with all thy mind. This is the first and great commandment. And the second is like unto it, Thou shalt love thy neighbor as thyself. On these two commandments hang all the law and the prophets" (Matt. 22:35-40).

This is the "great" original law, given in two divisions: (1) love to God; (2) love to man. Christ did not quote the Decalogue, for these commandments are not in the Decalogue, but he went back to the fountainhead of all truth.

Now, this perfect love—Godward and manward—was the original law of man's being. It was "first," both in importance and in point of time. The new covenant restores to us in perfection this divine principle; for when the law of God is written in our hearts we are "made perfect in love" (I John 4:18); "God dwelleth in us, and his love is perfected in us" (vs. 12). "The love of God is shed abroad in our hearts by the Holy Ghost which is given unto us" (Rom. 5:5). So complete, so perfect, is this moral principle within, that the Apostle exclaims, "Love is the fulfilling of the law" (13:10). Love is the "more excellent way" of the gospel (I Cor. 12:31; 13).

Objective Law

"On these two commandments [comprising the *one* original law of love] hang all the law and the prophets" (Matt. 22:40). The Decalogue was not that original law; it was not "first"; it was only *hung on* that law. "All the law and the prophets" did not constitute that higher law, but were only later additions. In other words, all objective revelation of whatever form or nature is not that original law, but is *only an expression of that higher law, adapted to human conditions.* Therefore the New Testament itself, as a book, is not that law, but only an expression of it, adapted to the present condition of things. Baptism, the Lord's Supper, foot washing, healing of the sick, caring for the poor and needy, and other things contained in it are clearly limited to the present order and are not adapted to the angels or to the redeemed saints in the heavenly world hereafter. For this reason, as I have previously shown, divine revelation has been of necessity progressive; and this also explains why some things commanded of God in one age of the world have been withdrawn at a later date; and why an entire system, like the Mosaic, has been abolished and superseded by another and better system. "There is made of necessity a change also of the law" (Heb. 7:12).

The design of objective revelation, then, is to exhibit the divine principle of love to God and to man. In the Mosaic dispensation this was accomplished (as well as could be done through sinful men) by means of an elaborate politico-religious system adapted to that age. But in the gospel dispensation the law of perfect love is placed in the very hearts of the redeemed; therefore, no coercive law is necessary in order to secure its manifestation. "If a man love me, he will keep my words," says Jesus (John 14:23). Pure love flows out spontaneously to God our Creator and to all men, even our enemies. This is "righteousness and true holiness."

Moral Law

This original, universal law of holiness is *world law*. Moral law exists in the nature of things; whereas a law that must first be made by external authority, or command, in order to become a law at all, is not a moral law. Therefore all laws of God that have originated by his command or decree are ceremonial; for in order to become laws at all they had to be first revealed objectively to man. On the other hand, all moral law existed subjectively in man originally; and this primitive writing, as we have shown, has to a great extent remained in him until the present day and is restored to its perfect condition in Bible holiness.

Ceremonial Holiness

Since "righteousness and true holiness" describes man's inward, moral nature originally and also in redemption, it is evident that holiness in its true sense belongs exclusively to him, so far as earthly objects are concerned. It is noteworthy that under the new covenant this term is applied, almost without exception, to the redeemed person. No external things can be holy in this moral, or true, sense.

The holiness of *things,* so often referred to, especially in the Old Testament, never could be more than a mere external, ceremonial holiness, a sort of consecration, or dedication, to a religious use. No actual change was made in the nature of the things so dedicated. Thus, we read of "holy temple," "holy ark," "holy vessels," "holy altar," "holy veil," "holy Sabbath." None of these was holy in the nature of things, but at some time or other had to be made holy in order to become holy at all; therefore, these things were not moral in any respect, but were simply objects or observances ceremonially holy, made such by God's appointment or decree.

An Example of Ceremonial Holiness

In order to show the plain teachings of the Word and to make this subject entirely clear, I will select one particular example of ceremonial holiness—the Sabbath. This selection is made for two reasons: (1) because it furnishes material for illustrating the entire subject of ceremonial holiness; (2) be-

The Law of Holiness 153

cause of the particular emphasis on the Sabbath given by nearly all classes of Christians. I will consider the subject in chronological order—the seventh-day Sabbath first, and then the first-day Sabbath.

The Sabbath is classed again and again with all the other holy days, feasts, and ceremonial observances of the Law, *heading the list of sacred days* (Num. 28; Lev. 23:1-3; I Chron. 23:31; II Chron. 2:4; 8:13; 31:3; Neh. 10:33). On these holy seventh-day Sabbaths all the other "holy" things of the Law were brought into use—priesthood, altar, vessels, tabernacle, sacrifices. Hence, in harmony with this general classification, the Sabbath stands in the Decalogue, "the covenant," as the representative of all other ceremonial observances.

Does the Sabbath rest upon the basis of nature, or simply upon divine appointment? "The sabbath was made for man" (Mark 2:27). Then, if God had not "made" it a holy Sabbath, it would never have been holy time; hence the sabbatic law was ceremonial, not moral; it is never termed "moral" in the Bible. There is nothing in nature to make one day different from another.

The Object of Law Ceremonies

All the ceremonial observances of the Law served a distinct purpose. In Colossians 2, where they are summed up as holy days, new moons, and Sabbath days, Paul says they "are a shadow of things to come; but the body is of Christ" (vss. 16-17). This shows that they occupy a typical relation. The writer of Hebrews represents the Law as "having a shadow of good things to come, and not the very image of the things" thus foreshadowed (10:1). Some ceremonies of the Law served a double purpose, being memorials of past events as well as types of something future. For example, the Passover, which commemorated the miraculous preservation of the Hebrews from death when the first born were slain in Egypt, also pointed forward to "Christ our passover . . . sacrificed for us" (I Cor. 5:7). Likewise, the Sabbath had a sort of threefold signification: (1) it commemorated the deliverance of Israel from Egyptian bondage, and (2) God's rest at the close of the creative period; (3) it was also a "shadow of things to come," meeting a fulfillment under the gospel of Christ, as we shall now see.

Paul names the Sabbath as one of the things that were "a shadow of things to come" (Col. 2:17). What can the Sabbath typify? It must symbolize something in another department that bears a certain analogy to it. Where shall we look for its fulfillment? Let us first observe its position in the type, then we can tell exactly where to look for its position and signification in the antitype. The Sabbath was inscribed on the tables that were placed in the ark. This is set forth in the Scriptures as representative of the new covenant laws *in our hearts* in the gospel age (Heb. 8:9-10). Therefore, the antitype of the Sabbath is also in our hearts. It cannot represent another literal Sabbath, for that would destroy the true relation of type and antitype. Besides, a literal day cannot be written in a person's heart. Not one of the Old Testament ceremonies represented literal ceremonies under the gospel, but every one met a *spiritual* fulfillment; accordingly, the Sabbath commandment must also reach its fulfillment antitypically in something *spiritual* in the heart. The literal Sabbath was bodily rest; the spiritual sabbath is—what? *Soul rest.* Praise the Lord! Our great Redeemer, who has established the new covenant, said: "Come unto me, all ye that labor and are heavy laden and I will give you rest. . . . And ye shall find rest unto your souls" (Matt. 11:28-29). "His rest shall be glorious," exclaimed the prophet (Isa. 11:10), and all the blood-washed can reply that it is even so.

Consider Hebrews 4:4-10. The following facts appear so clear in this passage that they cannot be overlooked:

1. *The Israelites, with their seventh-day Sabbath, did not obtain true rest.*

2. *Those who entered Canaan under Joshua did not obtain it* after they were established in Canaan.

3. *David prophesied concerning "another day,"* interpreted by the inspired writer as the gospel day, which came "after so long a time."

4. *"Today"*—the gospel day—*"there remaineth therefore a rest* ["the keeping of a sabbath," margin] *to the people of God."*

5. *This rest, or sabbath, is spiritual* in its nature, for it is ob-

tained by faith—"We which have believed do enter into rest"
(vs. 3).

6. *This spiritual rest, or sabbath, is the direct antitype of the
seventh-day Sabbath:* "For he that is entered into his rest, he
also hath ceased from his own works, as God did from his" (vs.
10). Notice carefully this sixth point. When God ceased the
work of creation, he ceased once for all. Likewise, in obtaining
this spiritual sabbath, we cease perpetually from our own
works, as God did from his. This makes our sabbath a perpetual
one. Our "own works," from which we must cease forever in
order to enter into this rest that "remaineth to the people of
God," include everything that is contrary to rest—self, self-
efforts, sins, and all. It is by faith that we "enter into rest."

Reader, the true sabbath of the gospel dispensation is not the
observance of any literal day. We have a perpetual sabbath, a
rest to the soul.

Since our sins are all gone and we have indeed "entered into
his rest," we are able to "serve him without fear, in holiness
and righteousness before him, all the days of our life" (Luke
1: 74-75). Every day is a day of holiness to the true Christian,
because in the gospel dispensation holiness is not attached to
one day out of seven, but pertains to the man himself; and he
must live holily *every day in the week.* And when he really
understands the subject, he "esteemeth every day alike" (Rom.
14: 5), so far as moral things and holiness are concerned.

New Testament Ceremonies

The new covenant, while placed in the hearts of God's people,
is not to be hidden there. We have a particular relationship
with each other and with a world of sinners. For this reason
God has seen fit to give us in this dispensation a system of ceremonial observances designed as channels of expression, through
which we manifest openly our redemption, faith, love, hope,
and the spontaneous worship of our hearts.

The ceremonial observances of the gospel, however, do not
possess the rigidity of the Law system. Peter describes that
system as "a yoke upon the neck of the disciples, which neither
our fathers nor we were able to bear" (Acts 15: 10). The ceremonies of Christ are no such yoke as that, but they are a yoke,

nevertheless. "It is good for a man that he bear the yoke in his youth" (Lam. 3:27). Jesus says, "Take my yoke upon you" (Matt. 11:29). There are obligations under the new covenant dispensation, and these we must take. The Lord, however, has given us this comforting assurance: "My yoke is easy, and my burden is light" (vs. 30).

Special reasons for New Testament ceremonies were given in chapters 13, 14, and 15 (particularly in chapter 15, under the subhead, "The Purpose of Ordinances"), hence a brief reference to the three ordinances will be sufficient in this place.

Four specific things experienced and enjoyed by the new covenant believer require open and public manifestation:

1. *Our individual salvation*—our personal acceptance of Christ and the authority and law of his kingdom is declared openly in the rite of water baptism.

2. *The procuring cause of redemption*—the ground of all salvation, and the basis of our hopes, present and future, is the atonement. The Lord's Supper, or Communion, is the outward symbol of this.

3. *The depth of that true and special love* which exists between us as the real disciples of Christ—Christ's "new commandment. . . . That ye love one another; as I have loved you" (John 13:34)—is outwardly and visibly expressed by the ordinance of foot washing, as shown in chapter 15 of this work.

4. *Our worship and our faith.* The worship, praise, and devotion experienced by every saved believer requires external expression, and the faith of the gospel by which he has been saved must be preached to all men, as Christ has commanded; therefore the necessity of public worship. It is certainly in accordance with the law of Christ that his people should at intervals gather together in his name (Matt. 18:20). In order to do this they must have a *place* and a *time* to assemble. That the apostolic church had regular public services is shown by the Scriptures. "Not forsaking the assembling of ourselves together, as the manner of some is" (Heb. 10:25).

If it is necessary that there be in the Christian dispensation an institution to commemorate the great fact of Christ's death, then it is positively necessary that there also be something to commemorate the greatest of all events—his resurrection. For "if Christ be not risen, then is our preaching vain, and your faith is also vain" (I Cor. 15:14). All the New Testament institutions are distinctively Christian; not one is borrowed from the old dispensation. And if the Sabbath was given to commemorate the completion of natural creation, how appropriate that the day of Christian worship should commemorate the resurrection of Christ, who thus stands at the head of the new and spiritual creation!

The first meeting of the disciples after the resurrection took place on the first day of the week (John 20:19-20).

The second meeting was just one week later (vs. 26).

A little later we have the mention of a notable meeting of the church. "And when the day of Pentecost was fully come, they were all with one accord in one place" (Acts 2:1). Pentecost came on the morrow after the Jewish Sabbath (Lev. 23:15-16), therefore it was on Sunday, the first day of the week.

Another meeting of the Christian church on Sunday is mentioned as taking place at Troas, in Asia Minor. "Upon the first day of the week, when the disciples came together to break bread, Paul preached unto them" (Acts 20:7). Here we have the Communion service on the first day. Now, this meeting did not occur just because the Apostle happened to be there that day, for he was there a number of days (vs. 6). But on the first day of the week they came together, and the facts and the language fairly imply that they were in the habit of doing this—"Upon the first day of the week, when the disciples came together to break bread."

In the second century we find Justin Martyr saying: "And on the day called Sunday, all who live in cities or in the country gather together to one place, and the memoirs of the apostles or the writings of the prophets are read, as long as time permits. . . . And they who are well-to-do, and willing, give what each thinks fit; and what is collected is deposited with the president, who succors the orphans and widows, and those who . . . are in want."—*First Apology of Justin,* Chap. LXVII

The day of the resurrection was so glorious to the Christian church that it was ever afterwards called "the Lord's day." And it is appropriately thus designated. "The Lord's Supper," commemorating his death, is distinctively Christian; therefore the day of worship, commemorating his resurrection, must be "the Lord's day." "I was in the Spirit on the Lord's day" (Rev. 1:10). All subsequent Christians called Sunday "the Lord's day."

That Sunday was intended to be the worship day of the Christian church is further shown by the fact that God himself placed his approval and seal upon it by making it the day of divine revelation, both to the church itself and to the world. On that day Christ revealed himself and the startling fact of his resurrection to the assembled disciples (John 20:19). On that day he revealed himself specifically to Thomas, one of the Twelve (vss. 26-29). On that day the Holy Ghost dispensation began; the Holy Spirit himself was revealed to the sons of men in a new capacity; the church was ordained and set in order, clothed with the gifts of the Spirit. On that day the Apostle John in the Isle of Patmos was "in the Spirit" and received the wonderful visions of the Apocalypse. *Every new, special, and glorious thing on record that God made known to the Apostles in the new dispensation was revealed on the first day of the week.* It is "the Lord's day," and therefore it was the Lord's revelation day.

From this fountainhead of regular weekly worship on the first day of the week, established by Christ and the Apostles, we can easily trace in a continual stream the same custom during all the ages.

Perversion of New Testament Ceremonies

Originally, the Lord's day was simply a day of worship. The day itself possessed no more holiness than any other day; therefore the true Christians, in full light, esteemed "every day alike" in this respect (Rom. 14:5), though assembling together for worship on the first day of the week, as I have shown. Later, however, when the great apostasy began, and men began to lose sight of true spiritual things, they also began to attach more and more importance to external things and attribute to them the greatest degree of holiness and veneration. In this manner the simple worship day of the Christians became idolized as a holy Sabbath day in the place of the Jewish Sabbath of the old dispensation.

Shall we change our day of worship from the example set by the Apostles, simply because of these extremes concerning Sunday keeping and Sunday holiness? No! The same apostasy perverted other institutions of the gospel as well. The Catholic priest takes the bread and the wine and (as Romanists say) converts these elements into the actual body and blood of the Lord, then falls down and worships them. Some Protestants also have adopted nearly the same belief and practice.

If people desire to worship the bread in the sacrament or to worship Sunday as a sacred Sabbath day, that is their own responsibility. But we should take the same things and use them in the Bible way, because they are useful and necessary. The bread and the wine in the Communion do not differ in their nature from other elements of the same kind; they are merely put to a different use. So also the Lord's day is the same to us as are all other days, except in this, that, following the apostolic example, we put it to a different use. Morally, there is no difference. No New Testament ordinance or ceremony is termed "holy." New Testament holiness is *"true holiness"* (Eph. 4:24) and pertains not to things, but to redeemed men and women.

"Brethren, ye have been called unto liberty; only use not liberty for an occasion to the flesh, but by love serve one another" (Gal. 5:13). Freedom from legal bondage, however, must not be allowed to cause us to take extreme positions— positions that will rob us of the true spirit of worship and devotion on the first day of the week, or that will lead us to ignore or trample on the religious convictions of other sincere, conscientious Christians. We must learn well to practice the lesson of Romans 14:1-6, so that, though we "esteem every day alike," we can patiently bear with, and "despise not," the one who is so "weak in the faith" that he "esteemeth one day above another." Paul set a good example: "Unto the Jews I became as a Jew, that I might gain the Jews." This he did for the sake of his influence and for the sake of the cause of Christ.

Chapter 23

THE KINGDOM OF GOD

The subject of the kingdom of God has been strongly emphasized by many people. Visionists have dreamed of a coming age of blessedness and earthly glory, while writers and orators have described it in loftiest phrase and by highly colored word pictures, the creations of their own fancy. My purpose, however, is not to set forth a mere theory, no matter how desirable or captivating it may appear, but to show what the Bible clearly teaches concerning the subject, when all forced and fanciful interpretations are omitted.

The Kingdom in Prophecy

During the Babylonian captivity of the Jews, King Nebuchadnezzar had a dream that directly concerns the subject of the divine kingdom. "Thou, O king, sawest, and behold a great image. This great image, whose brightness was excellent, stood before thee; and the form thereof was terrible. This image's head was of fine gold, his breast and his arms of silver, his belly and his thighs of brass, his legs of iron, his feet part of iron and part of clay. Thou sawest till that a stone was cut out without hands, which smote the image upon his feet that were of iron and clay, and break them to pieces. Then was the iron, the clay, the brass, the silver, and the gold broken to pieces together, and became like the chaff of the summer threshing floors; and the wind carried them away, that no place was found for them: and the stone that smote the image became a great mountain, and filled the whole earth" (Dan. 2: 31-35).

Having made known the dream itself, Daniel proceeded to show its meaning: "This is the dream; and we will tell the interpretation thereof before the king. Thou, O king, art a king of kings: for the God of heaven hath given thee a kingdom, power, and strength, and glory. And wheresoever the children of men dwell, the beasts of the field and the fowls of the heaven hath he given into thine hand, and hath made thee ruler over them all. Thou art this head of gold" (vss. 36-38).

The head of gold represented the Babylonian Empire. Though Daniel addressed the king as this head, yet it is evident that the real signification is the empire itself; for, as we shall see, each of the remaining divisions of this image is treated, not as an individual king, but as a universal empire. At this time the Babylonian kingdom was in the height of its power and glory under Nebuchadnezzar.

"And after thee shall arise another kingdom inferior to thee" (vs. 39). This signifies the Medo-Persian Empire, which conquered Babylon about 538 B.C. and became the second universal empire. "In that night was Belshazzar the king of the Chaldeans slain. And Darius the Median took the kingdom" (5: 30-31).

"And another third kingdom of brass, which shall bear rule over all the earth" (2: 39). This signifies the Grecian Empire which, under Alexander the Great, conquered the Persian Empire and became the ruling empire.

"And the fourth kingdom shall be strong as iron: forasmuch as iron breaketh in pieces and subdueth all things: and as iron that breaketh all these, shall it break in pieces and bruise. And whereas thou sawest the feet and toes, part of potters' clay, and part of iron, the kingdom shall be divided; but there shall be in it of the strength of the iron, forasmuch as thou sawest the iron mixed with miry clay. And as the toes of the feet were part of iron and part of clay, so the kingdom shall be partly strong, and partly broken. And whereas thou sawest iron mixed with miry clay, they shall mingle themselves with the seed of men: but they shall not cleave one to another, even as iron is not mixed with clay" (2: 40-43). This signifies the Roman Empire, which conquered the Greeks and established itself as the ruling power of the world. This description of Rome includes both her strong and her divided condition, but it is all summed up under the one head—"fourth kingdom."

"And in the days of these kings shall the God of heaven set up a kingdom, which shall never be destroyed: and the kingdom shall not be left to other people, but it shall break in pieces and consume all these kingdoms, and it shall stand forever. Forasmuch as thou sawest that the stone was cut out of the mountain without hands, and that it brake in pieces the iron, the brass, the clay, the silver, and the gold; the great God hath made known to the king what shall come to pass hereafter: and the dream is certain, and the interpretation thereof sure" (vss. 44-45).

According to this prophecy, the stone which was "cut out without hands" represents the kingdom of God as the fifth universal kingdom; and since it smote the fourth division of the image, we must therefore look to the time of the reign of the Roman Empire for the establishment of the kingdom of God.

The same four kingdoms are represented in Daniel 7 by four consecutive beasts. "These great beasts, which are four, are four kings, which shall arise out of the earth. But the saints of the most High shall take the kingdom, and possess the kingdom forever, even forever and ever" (vss. 17-18). Here again the kingdom of God is represented as number five, in contrast with the four.

Established by Christ

The prophet Isaiah also clearly predicts the establishment of this kingdom of God, and he also informs us by whom it is to be established, and *when*. "For unto us a child is born, unto us a son is given: and the government shall be upon his shoulder: and his name shall be called Wonderful, Counselor, The mighty God, The everlasting Father, The Prince of Peace. Of the increase of his government and peace there shall be no end, upon the throne of David, and upon his kingdom, to order it, and to establish it with judgment and with justice from henceforth even forever" (Isa. 9:6-7).

Now, when this "child is born," when this "son is given," the one who is The mighty God, The Prince of Peace, he will establish "his kingdom" "with judgment and with justice," and "of the increase of his government and peace there shall be no end." Every Bible student knows that this refers to Christ. However, let us seal it with the Word. The angel Gabriel said to Mary, a virgin of Nazareth: "Thou shalt conceive in thy womb, and bring forth a son, and shalt call his name JESUS. He shall be great, and shall be called the Son of the

Highest: and the Lord God shall give unto him the throne of his father David; and he shall reign over the house of Jacob forever; and of his kingdom there shall be no end" (Luke 1: 31-33).

Some people are looking for the kingdom of God to come in some future age, but these Scripture passages clearly locate its initial manifestation at the first advent of Christ. It was when he was born into the world as a "son" that he became a king and established his kingdom. He himself taught this during his ministry. When on trial before Pilate, he acknowledged that he had a kingdom, but said, "My kingdom is not of this world. . . . Pilate therefore said unto him, Art thou a king then? Jesus answered, Thou sayest that I am a king. To this end was I born, and for this cause came I into the world" (John 18: 36-37). We must therefore look to his first coming as the time for the establishment of the kingdom. "Now after that John was put in prison, Jesus came into Galilee, preaching the gospel of the kingdom of God, and saying, the time is fulfilled, and the kingdom of God is at hand: repent ye, and believe the gospel" (Mark 1: 14-15).

This is in exact accordance with the prophecy of Daniel already given. The "stone" smote the fourth, or Roman, division of the image. So also it was in the day of the Roman Empire that the Christ child appeared. When this humble babe was born in the city of Bethlehem, Rome was in the height of her glory, ruled by her proud monarch, Augustus Caesar. But the kingdom Christ was to establish was destined to overthrow all the kingdoms of pagan darkness and to stand forever.

This kingdom of God on earth was represented concretely by the church of God, and it soon came into conflict with all the vile powers of heathenism enthroned in the Roman Empire. This we have seen and described in chapter 16. That the application is correct is shown by Revelation 12, where the woman, representing the early church, is opposed by the "great red dragon, having seven heads and ten horns" (vs. 3). This great dragon, which is easily identified by its heads and horns, symbolizes the Roman Empire under its pagan form. Then appears the warfare of Christ and his angels against this dragon (vs. 7), by which is shown the early conflict of Christianity with paganism, "and the great dragon was cast out" (vs. 9). Christianity triumphed over heathenism. Listen! "And I heard a loud voice saying in heaven, Now is come salvation, and strength, and the kingdom of our God, and the power of his Christ: for the accuser of our brethren is cast down. . . . And they overcame him by the blood of the Lamb, and by the word of their testimony; and they loved not their lives unto the death" (vss. 10-11). How clearly this fulfills the prediction of Daniel 2 concerning the stone that smote the image!

The message of the kingdom of God was introduced by John. "In those days came John the Baptist, preaching in the wilderness of Judea, and saying, Repent ye: for the kingdom of heaven is at hand" (Matt. 3:1-2). Jesus bore witness to this work of John by saying, "The law and the prophets were until John: since that time the kingdom of God is preached, and every man presseth into it" (Luke 16:16). The same message was taken up by Christ, "preaching the gospel of the kingdom of God, and saying, The time is fulfilled, and the kingdom of God is at hand: repent ye, and believe the gospel" (Mark 1:14-15).

Many teachers who have accepted the theory of a coming earthly kingdom find it difficult indeed to evade the force of all these Scripture passages that so clearly point to the first advent of Christ as the time of the establishment of his kingdom. In order to save their theory, some of them try to make a distinction between the kingdom of heaven and the kingdom of God, saying that one was given when Christ appeared the first time, but that the other is reserved for his second coming. Now, the object of this book is not to combat every theory of men, but to show what the Bible teaches. This I shall do in this case by showing that the New Testament makes no distinction between the kingdom of heaven and the kingdom of God, but *applies both expressions to the same thing.*

John preached, "The kingdom of heaven is at hand" (Matt. 3:2). "The law and the prophets were until John: since that time the kingdom of God is preached" (Luke 16:16).

"Blessed are the poor in spirit: for theirs is the kingdom of heaven" (Matt. 5:3). "Blessed be ye poor: for yours is the kingdom of God" (Luke 6:20).

Jesus said concerning John: "He that is least in the kingdom of heaven is greater than he" (Matt. 11:11); "He that is least in the kingdom of God is greater than he" (Luke 7:28).

"It is given unto you to know the mysteries of the kingdom of heaven" (Matt. 13:11). "Unto you it is given to know the mystery of the kingdom of God" (Mark 4:11).

"The kingdom of heaven is like to a grain of mustard seed" (Matt. 13:31). "Whereunto shall we liken the kingdom of God? . . . It is like a grain of mustard seed" (Mark 4:30-31).

"The kingdom of heaven is like unto leaven, which a woman took, and hid in three measures of meal" (Matt. 13:33). "Whereunto shall I liken the kingdom of God? It is like leaven, which a woman took and hid in three measures of meal" (Luke 13:20-21).

"Jesus said unto his disciples, . . . A rich man shall hardly enter into the kingdom of heaven. And again I say unto you, It is easier for a camel to go through the eye of a needle, than for a rich man to enter into the kingdom of God" (Matt. 19:23-24).

The kingdom of heaven and the kingdom of God are the same thing.

The Nature of Christ's Kingdom

Jesus said, "My kingdom is not of this world" (John 18:36). Earthly kingdoms are of one nature; the kingdom of God is of another. We can determine the nature of God's kingdom on earth by what the Scriptures have to say about it.

1. *It is a doctrine.* "Go thou and preach the kingdom of God" (Luke 9:60). "The kingdom of God is preached, and every man presseth into it" (16:16). The entire message of the gospel is "preaching the things concerning the kingdom of God" (Acts 8:12). In some manner the kingdom of God is so contained in, and expressed by, the gospel that the preaching of that gospel is called the preaching of the kingdom of God.

2. *It is an experience.* This is indicated by the fact that we are commanded to seek for it. "Seek ye first the kingdom of God, and his righteousness" (Matt. 6:33). "The kingdom of God is preached, and every man presseth into it" (Luke 16:16). This shows that it is an experience to be obtained by earnest

effort. It is spiritual in its nature (17:20-21). What a clear contrast between the nature of Christ's kingdom and that of earthly kingdoms! Earthly kingdoms are introduced with great external pomp and display; but Jesus says, "My kingdom is not of this world." It is not "here" or "there," for it is not subject to any particular geographical definition or limitation, but is spiritual in its nature and "within you," that is, if you have earnestly sought it according to Christ's command and "pressed into it."

3. *It is the present inheritance of the saints.* In the very first century of Christian grace John testified that he was "in the kingdom and patience of Jesus Christ" (Rev. 1:9). Paul instructs the Colossians to give "thanks unto the Father, which hath made us meet to be partakers of the inheritance of the saints in light: who hath delivered us from the power of darkness, and hath translated us into the kingdom of his dear Son" (Col. 1:12-13). "For the kingdom of God is not meat and drink; but righteousness, and peace, and joy in the Holy Ghost" (Rom. 14:17).

4. *It is a visible working force.* "I tell you of a truth, there be some standing here, which shall not taste of death, till they see the kingdom of God" (Luke 9:27). (See also Mark 9:1.) It is evident that another phase of the kingdom is here set forth; for as a doctrine it had already been preached; as an experience, some had already sought it and pressed into it. But here is a distinct, visible phase that was to be manifested during the lifetime of some who were then present and heard the words of Christ. This phase of the kingdom is identical with the church of God as a visible, working force in the world, and on the Day of Pentecost, when the church was set in order and dedicated by an outpouring of the Holy Spirit, the followers of Jesus saw the kingdom of God come with power (Luke 24:49.)

A Reign on the Earth*

In this organic form the kingdom of God shone forth gloriously in the morning of this dispensation. In the visions of the

*This subject merits, and in fact really demands, a much more thorough treatment than is possible within the limits of this work. For a detailed study of the prophetic aspects of this theme, see *The Revelation Explained*, and *Prophetic Lectures on Daniel and the Revelation.* (Out of print.)

Apocalypse, John saw this blessed triumphal reign of the saints on earth; for at the very opening of the plan of salvation by Christ, the redeemed took up the new song of redemption (Rev. 5:9-10). This does not refer to some future earth reign; it describes the reign of righteousness enjoyed by the people of God on earth at the very beginning of the gospel dispensation. They were already kings and priests unto God (I Pet. 2:9). Paul declares that "they which receive abundance of grace and of the gift of righteousness shall reign in life by one, Jesus Christ" (Rom. 5:17). This "reign on the earth" was a real, public one, coexistent and coextensive with the triumph of the apostolic church itself. It was when the church conquered paganism that the cry went up, "Now is come salvation, and strength, and the kingdom of our God, and the power of his Christ" (Rev. 12:10).

A Reign with Christ

But this phase of the kingdom, which is identical with the visible church in its organic form, was not to continue thus. In order to understand the teaching of the Scriptures concerning the kingdom subsequent to its establishment, we must understand the teaching concerning the church subsequent to its establishment. In chapter 16 we showed from Revelation 12 that the church is set forth under a double symbol—a woman and her son—in order to show two phases of her existence during the Apostasy. The phase represented by the man-child, who was "caught up unto God, and to his throne," is that phase of the church which was cut off from the earth through martyrdom and persecution; the phase represented by the woman who "fled into the wilderness" is that phase of the church which continued on earth, but was hidden in the great apostasy. With these thoughts in mind we shall approach the twentieth chapter of Revelation.

Here nothing is said about the woman in the wilderness, but the narrative takes up the other phase (the man-child), which was caught up to God and there lived and reigned. "And I saw thrones, and they sat upon them, and judgment was given unto them: and I saw the souls of them that were beheaded for the witness of Jesus, and for the word of God, and which had not worshiped the beast, neither his image, neither had received his mark upon their foreheads, or in their hands; and they lived and reigned with Christ a thousand years" (vs. 4). Notice carefully the facts:

1. It was the "souls of them that were beheaded for the witness of Jesus" that "reigned with Christ."

2. Not one word is said about people being literally resurrected and reigning. This reign was *before the resurrection of the literal dead,* for the resurrection of these did not take place until after the thousand years, at the end of this series of prophecy, and it includes both classes, good and bad; for some are found written in the book of life, while some are not (vss. 11-15).

3. There is no reign on the earth mentioned here at all; the reign was "with Christ." How well this agrees with Paul's statement, "I am in a strait betwixt two, having a desire to depart, and to be with Christ; which is far better: nevertheless to abide in the flesh is more needful for you" (Phil. 1:23-24).

The First Resurrection

"But the rest of the dead lived not again until the thousand years were finished. This is the first resurrection. Blessed and holy is he that hath part in the first resurrection: on such the second death hath no power, but they shall be priests of God and of Christ, and shall reign with him a thousand years" (Rev. 20:5-6).

Here we have a resurrection to life that is called the "first resurrection," but notice (vs. 5) that this first resurrection is represented as taking place *after* the one thousand years: "But the rest of the dead lived not again until the thousand years were finished. *This* is the first resurrection." It is both before and after the thousand years, and still is all *before* the literal resurrection at Christ's second coming, when "the dead, small and great, stand before God" (vs. 12). In the following chapter I shall show by many texts that are not involved in prophetic interpretations that there is but one literal resurrection of the dead and that both the righteous and the wicked will be raised at the same time. What, then, is the "first resurrection"?

The first resurrection makes men "blessed and holy." According to the Scriptures, men must receive a spiritual resurrection, or quickening, before they can be made holy; for they are represented as "dead in trespasses and in sins" (Eph. 2:1). "And you, being dead in your sins . . . hath he quickened together with him, having forgiven you all trespasses" (Col. 2:13). That the act of salvation, which makes us alive in Christ, is scripturally "the first resurrection" is proved most positively by the words of Christ himself: "Verily, verily, I say unto you, The hour is coming, and now is, when the dead shall hear the voice of the Son of God: and they that hear shall live" (John 5:25). "We know that we have passed from death unto life" (I John 3:14).

In Revelation 20 the people of God who have had "part in the first resurrection" are brought to view as two great companies: those *before* the period of the thousand years, and the remainder—symbolized by "the rest of the dead" (vs. 5)—*after* the close of that period. Such have been the facts. A great host of people were saved before the great apostasy, and since then another mighty host is being quickened into spiritual life, but it is all "the first resurrection," as verses 5 and 6 show.

Another "Reign on the Earth"

In Revelation 20:8-9 the subject is not the reign of the martyrs in paradise, but once more we have in prominence "the camp of the saints" "on the breadth of the earth." Here we have the mighty host who have had "part in the first resurrection" *after the close of the thousand-year period,* reigning in triumph and victory while the powers of evil are gathered together for the final conflict. The scene is brought to a close by the second coming of Christ, the literal resurrection of the dead, and the general judgment (vss. 10-15).

That the reign of God's people on earth is divided into two distinct periods is shown also by other prophecies. Daniel 7 records a vision of four great beasts, symbolizing the Babylonian, Medo-Persian, Grecian, and Roman empires. Verse 18, in connection with Daniel 2:31-44 (already discussed in this chapter), shows that the saints were to possess the kingdom of God before the overthrow of these four kingdoms. These prophecies were fulfilled by the establishment of Christianity by Christ during the reign of the Roman Empire. Then, under the symbol of a "little horn" out of the fourth beast, follows a description of the Papacy, which was to "wear out the saints of the most High" for a period of 1,260 years (7:19-25).

Beginning with the Sixteenth Century Reformation, and continuing during the Protestant Era, spiritual reformations from time to time have brought judgment against that beast power which had for ages worn out the "saints of the most High." In these spiritual reformations many people were resurrected to spiritual life in Christ. But a little later, under the fourth ecclesiastical epoch, that of the pure church restored, the real spiritual reign of the saints is restored also in the pure gospel light of the evening time; and now the remainder of Daniel's prophecy is fulfilled, which says, "And the kingdom and dominion, and the greatness of the kingdom under the whole heaven, shall be given to the people of the saints of the most High, whose kingdom is an everlasting kingdom" (7:27).

"Fear not, little flock; for it is your Father's good pleasure to give you the kingdom" (Luke 12:32). The little stone of Nebuchadnezzar's vision will yet "become a great mountain" and fill the "whole earth."

The Universal Kingdom

Thus far we have considered the subject of the kingdom of God chiefly from the standpoint of Christ's spiritual work on the earth, either in the hearts of his people, as a spiritual experience, or in his visible church. But there is another distinct phase that we must understand in order to harmonize all the facts. This is the universal phase. Christ is now universal King, Lord of heaven and earth. Before his ascension he claimed this dominion, saying, "All power is given unto me in heaven and in earth" (Matt. 28:18). This universal dominion is expressed by Paul thus: "Which he wrought in Christ, when he raised him from the dead, and set him at his own right hand in the heavenly places, far above all principality, and power, and might, and dominion, and every name that is named, not only in this world, but also in that which is to come: and hath put all things under his feet, and gave him to be the head over all things" (Eph. 1:20-22).

Peter describes Christ's universal reign thus: "Who is gone into heaven, and is on the right hand of God; angels and authorities and powers being made subject unto him" (I Pet. 3:22). Christ is now "King of kings, and Lord of lords."

Viewed from this standpoint, the earth as a whole "is the Lord's, and the fullness thereof; the world, and they that dwell therein" (Ps. 24:1). The whole earth and universe are his kingdom; therefore all sinners and evil men are in his (universal) kingdom, but they exist as rebels against his throne, dominion, and authority. But this will not always continue. Christ cannot long endure in his universal kingdom those who rebel against his law; therefore at his second coming "the Son of man shall send forth his angels, and they shall gather out of his kingdom all things that offend, and them which do iniquity; and shall cast them into a furnace of fire: there shall be wailing and gnashing of teeth. Then shall the righteous shine forth as the sun in the kingdom of their Father" (Matt. 13:41-43).

This is the end of earthly things, when Christ will be revealed from heaven at the last day, when the wicked will be banished forever from the universe of God's dwelling, and our Lord will be "glorified in his saints," who will be received into heaven itself. (See II Thess. 1:7-10.) Then the present spiritual phase of the earthly kingdom will be swallowed up in the great universal kingdom, and thus there will be ministered to us an abundant entrance "into the everlasting kingdom of our Lord and Savior Jesus Christ" (II Pet. 1:11).

Now notice carefully the facts as brought forth heretofore and as clearly stated in I Corinthians 15:22-28:

1. *Christ is now universal King.*
2. *"He must reign"*—continue to reign—*"till he hath put all his enemies under his feet."*
3. *"The last enemy that shall be destroyed is death."* Now, this destruction will be accomplished by the resurrection, but the entire reign of Christ is to take place *before* this resurrection; for death is "the last enemy" that he will conquer. Then "he shall have put down all rule and all authority and power."

What, then, takes place at the time of the resurrection and the destruction of the "last enemy"? "Then the end." (The word "cometh" is not in the original.) "Then . . . the end, when he shall have delivered up the kingdom to God, even the Father" (vs. 24). The time when millennialists expect Christ to come, set up a kingdom, and *begin* to reign is the very time Paul points out as the *end* of Christ's personal redemptive reign, when he "shall have delivered up the kingdom to God."

Our Lord is now the reigning King of earth and heaven. At the cross he conquered sin; through his church he conquered paganism in the Roman Empire; through the Reformation he broke the power of the Papacy; through his pure church and restored kingdom he is now conquering the spiritual powers of darkness; and those who do not yield to the persuasive influences of his Spirit when manifested lovingly through a moral system, he will subdue by force and judgment at his coming, at which time "the last enemy"—death—shall be destroyed.

"And when all these things shall be subdued unto him, then shall the Son also himself be subject unto him that put all things under him, that God may be all in all" (vs. 28).*

---

*This bare outline may be supplemented by reference to the full discussion in *The Revelation Explained.*

CONCERNING THE DOCTRINE OF FINAL THINGS

Chapter 24

THE SECOND COMING OF CHRIST

After his resurrection from the dead Christ remained with his disciples many days, speaking of the things pertaining to the kingdom of God; then he led them out to Mount Olivet, near Bethany, and there gave them the final commission to preach in his name among all the nations. "And when he had spoken these things, while they beheld, he was taken up; and a cloud received him out of their sight. And while they looked steadfastly toward heaven as he went up, behold, two men stood by them in white apparel; which also said, Ye men of Galilee, why stand ye gazing up into heaven? this same Jesus, which is taken up from you into heaven, shall so come in like manner as ye have seen him go into heaven" (Acts 1:9-11). Christ had already informed them of his departure, but had said to them, "I will come again" (John 14:3).

In the New Testament much importance is attached to the second coming of Christ. The Scriptures uniformly point forward to that event as the time when the dead will be raised, when the general judgment will take place, and when final rewards will be meted out to the righteous and to the wicked. "The Son of man shall come in the glory of his Father with his angels; and then he shall reward every man according to his works" (Matt. 16:27). Paul clearly shows that the wicked "shall be punished with everlasting destruction," and the saints "glorified," "when the Lord Jesus shall be revealed from heaven with his mighty angels" (II Thess. 1: 7-11).

The End

"And as he sat upon the mount of Olives, the disciples came unto him privately, saying, Tell us, when shall these things be? and what shall be the sign of thy coming, and of the end of the world?" (Matt. 24:3). The burden of Matthew 24 shows that the disciples' question relates to the actual end of all earthly things, and this they associated in their question with the second coming. So also in I Corinthians 15, where Christ's coming and the resurrection are described, we read in this connection, "Then cometh the end" (vs. 24). This great event marks the end of time, the end of man's probation, the end of Christ's special redemptive reign—yea, as Peter says, "the end of all things is at hand" (I Pet. 4:7).

The Resurrection

So also the resurrection will take place at that time. "There shall be a resurrection of the dead, both of the just and unjust" (Acts 24:15). How many resurrections? One—"a resurrection." And this one resurrection of the dead is to include both the just and the unjust. The preceding chapter shows clearly that the prophecies which some people suppose refer to two literal resurrections teach no such thing. In this chapter we shall see that plain texts not involved in prophetic interpretations utterly preclude the idea of two literal resurrections in the future. In the present text it is simply "a resurrection," which includes both just and unjust.

This text does not state when the resurrection will take place, but Revelation 1:7 says: "Behold, he cometh with clouds; and every eye shall see him, and they also which pierced him: and all kindreds of the earth shall wail because of him." At his coming "every eye shall see him." This proves the fact of a general resurrection. That this resurrection includes the wicked also is shown by the statement that even those who "pierced him" will see him when he comes. The idea of two literal resurrections—one of the righteous and the other of the wicked—is utterly impossible according to this text.

That the resurrection is one, but includes both classes, is shown by the words of Christ himself (John 5:28-29). Both classes—good and bad—come forth from their graves in the same "hour."

Some think that I Thessalonians 4:16—"the dead in Christ shall rise first"—teaches two resurrections, but even a hasty examination should show that it teaches no such thing. The word "first" does not refer to other dead people at all. The text, with the context, simply shows that those who are living on the earth when Christ comes will not ascend to heaven *before* those who have died in Christ, but that the dead in Christ will rise *first*, and that then they will both ascend together.

So also Philippians 3:11—"If by any means I might attain unto the resurrection of the dead"—is sometimes perverted in order to sustain the false doctrine of two future literal resurrections of the dead; for, it is argued, if there were only one unconditional resurrection, Paul would not have sought to attain it. But the Bible represents the single resurrection of the dead as composed of *two classes,* the one receiving the resurrection unto eternal life, and the other a resurrection unto eternal damnation. The object and effort of Paul was to attain to this resurrection of life, which can be obtained only by proper effort, for it applies only to those who are saved.

When Lazarus was dead, Jesus said to Martha, "Thy brother shall rise again. Martha saith unto him, I know that he shall rise again in the resurrection at the last day" (John 11:23-24). Lazarus was a good man, and his sister had the idea that his resurrection would take place at the *last* day. Does this accord with the idea of two literal resurrections? The millennial idea of two resurrections places the resurrection of the righteous first and the resurrection of the wicked last—one thousand years later.

Where did Martha get this idea that the righteous would not be raised until the last day? Evidently from the words of Christ himself; for he affirms this four times in one chapter. "And this is the Father's will which hath sent me, that of all which he hath given me I should lose nothing, but should raise it up again at the last day. And . . . that every one which seeth the Son, and believeth on him, may have everlasting life: and I will raise him up at the last day" (John 6:39-40). "Whoso eateth my flesh, and drinketh my blood, hath eternal life; and I will raise him up at the last day" (vs. 54).

The General Judgment

To the Athenians Paul declared that God "hath appointed a day, in the which he will judge the world in righteousness by that man whom he hath ordained" (Acts 17:31). This judgment day is "the last day," the day of resurrection; for Paul says that "the Lord Jesus Christ . . . shall judge the quick and the dead at his appearing" (II Tim. 4:1). The Revelator connects the general judgment with the resurrection at the second coming. (See Rev. 20:11-13.)

Final Rewards

The doctrine of final rewards is naturally associated with the second coming and general judgment. "Behold, I come quickly; and my reward is with me, to give every man according as his work shall be" (Rev. 22:12). "For the Son of man shall come in the glory of his Father with his angels; and then he shall reward every man according to his works" (Matt. 16:27).

This will be the day of final rewards for all men. God has reserved the "unjust unto the day of judgment to be punished" (II Pet. 2:9). This will be an awful day, and one that we cannot escape. "Every eye shall see him" when he comes; for "the Lord Jesus shall be revealed from heaven with his mighty angels, in flaming fire taking vengeance on them that know not God, and that obey not the gospel of our Lord Jesus Christ: who shall be punished with everlasting destruction from the presence of the Lord, and from the glory of his power; when he shall come to be glorified in his saints" (II Thess. 1: 7-10). The same day that he is "glorified in his saints" will be the day of the everlasting banishment of the wicked.

The same great truth is also taught in Matthew 25 and centers in the second coming. "When the Son of man shall come in his glory, and all the holy angels with him, then shall he sit upon the throne of his glory: and before him shall be gathered all nations: and he shall separate them one from another, as a shepherd divideth his sheep from the goats: and he shall set the sheep on his right hand, but the goats on the left" (vss. 31-33). Here we have all men before the judgment throne *at the same time;* they are divided into two classes, represented by sheep and goats. This division is made for the purpose of settling their final destiny: "Then shall the King say unto them on his right hand, Come, ye blessed of my Father, inherit the kingdom prepared for you from the foundation of the world" (vs. 34). "Then shall he say also to them on the left hand, Depart from me, ye cursed, into everlasting fire, prepared for the devil and his angels" (vs. 41). Here we have the final destiny of both: "And these shall go away into everlasting punishment: but the righteous into life eternal" (vs. 46).

The Destruction of the Earth

The Word of God clearly teaches that the world which we now inhabit will be destroyed, pass away, and be no more. "Of old hast thou laid the foundation of the earth: and the heavens [aerial and planetary] are the work of thy hands. They shall perish . . . yea, all of them shall wax old like a garment; as a vesture shalt thou change them, and they shall be changed" (Ps. 102:25-26).

"Heaven and earth shall pass away," says Jesus (Matt. 24:35). Peter describes the manner in which the heavens and earth shall pass away. "The heavens" doubtless refers to the aerial heavens surrounding the earth. "But the heavens and the earth, which are now, by the same word are kept in store, reserved unto fire against the day of judgment and perdition of ungodly men" (II Pet. 3:7).

Notice that this destruction of the earth by fire is reserved till "the day of judgment and perdition of ungodly men." Millennialists have argued that the fire would come first and simply purify the earth, after which the righteous would reign here for a thousand years before the resurrection of the wicked. But according to Peter, the fire will not come until the time when the ungodly men shall receive their doom. Peter did not believe the millennial theory. He knew that when Christ came the end of all things pertaining to earth would take place and that the righteous and the wicked would be rewarded at the same time. Therefore he goes on to say: "But the day of the Lord will come as a thief in the night; in the which the heavens shall pass away with a great noise, and the elements shall melt with fervent heat, the earth also and the works that are therein shall be burned up. Seeing then that all these things shall be dissolved, what manner of persons ought ye to be in all holy conversation and godliness, looking for and hasting unto the coming of the day of God, wherein the heavens being on fire shall be dissolved, and the elements shall melt with fervent heat?" (vss. 10-12).

Peter does not say that the earth shall be burned over, but that it shall be "burned up"; that "all these things" shall "melt," be "dissolved," and "pass away." And in direct contrast he mentions a "new heavens and a new earth" (vs. 13), brought to view after the first one has gone. The Revelator also describes the passing of this old earth: "And I saw a great white throne, and him that sat on it, from whose face the earth and the heaven fled away; and there was found no place for them" (Rev. 20:11). Then in contrast he says, "And I saw a new heaven and a new earth: for the first heaven and the first earth were passed away; and there was no more sea" (21:1). This will be heaven, our future and eternal home.

The Premillennial Theory*

With these clear scriptural statements before us, we can readily see that there is no possibility of a millennium, or earthly reign of righteousness after Christ comes.

1. *There will be no time for a millennium.* The second coming of Christ, when he raises the dead and rewards the righteous, is "the last day." At that time "the mystery of God" will be finished, and there will be "time no longer" (Rev. 10:6-7). There is not a thousand years after the last day.

2. *There will be no place for a millennium.* As we have just seen, the destruction of the earth is to take place at the same time that the wicked are to be punished; and this destruction will be complete, the earth being "dissolved," "burned up," and passed away. Hence, there will be no earthly place for a millennium after Christ comes.

3. *There will be no need of an earthly millennium.* The offers of perfect salvation are all extended in the gospel dis-

---

*Only the briefest reference to millennialism is possible here. For an extensive historical account of the rise and development of the millennial doctrine, as well as a thorough scriptural and prophetic examination of its claims, see my book *Prophetic Lectures on Daniel and the Revelation,* pp. 178-253. (Out of print.)

pensation. "Behold, now is the accepted time; behold, now is the day of salvation" (II Cor. 6:2). Every means consistent with moral government and the moral freedom of the individual are now being employed to effect the salvation of men. Furthermore, since at the coming of Christ the wicked are judged and sent to their everlasting doom, there is positively no need of an earthly millennium.

The millenarian doctrine is delusive, both premillennial and postmillennial. The premillennial view in particular is presented in many forms, according to the fancies and desires of its propagators, but evidently the idea of both is about the same—that there will be an earthly kingdom and reign of Christ for one thousand years.

This theory was first introduced to Christianity by Cerinthus, who was the worst heretic of the first century. The church historian Eusebius has preserved a fragment of writing from Gaius, who lived in the second century, and who thus describes the doctrine of Cerinthus: "But Cerinthus, too, through revelations written, as he would have us believe, by a great apostle, brings before us marvelous things, which he pretends were shown him by angels; alleging that after the resurrection the kingdom of Christ is to be on earth, and that the flesh dwelling in Jerusalem is again to be subject to desires and pleasures. And being an enemy to the Scriptures of God, wishing to deceive men, he says that there is to be a space of a thousand years for marriage festivities."—*Ecclesiastical History*, III: 28

D. S. Warner said that the devil works especially to deceive men in either one of two ways: "Some other way than Christ, or some other time than now." This is true. If men will not accept Satan's deception that some other way will do, then he proceeds at once to delay all-important things until the future. Under certain forms of nonevangelical millennialism in particular, thousands of people have grasped the delusive idea that there will be after this dispensation another age of blessedness in which salvation will be effected. Such is a rank deception of the devil. "Now is the accepted time: behold, now is the day of salvation."

Chapter 25

THE DESTINY OF THE WICKED

The subject of the final destiny of those who persist in a life of wickedness has not been left to the mere opinions of men, but is a matter of revelation in the Christian Scriptures. Furthermore, our knowledge of the manner of God's dealings with sinful men in the past would lead us to conclude that at some time or other justice will be meted out to the guilty violators of his law.

They Will Be Punished

There is now in the world a large amount of perverse teaching and sentimental talk against the Bible doctrine of the punishment of the wicked. Hear the word of the Lord: "And it shall come to pass at that time that I will . . . punish the men that are settled on their lees: that say in their heart, The Lord will not do good, neither will he do evil" (Zeph. 1:12). This is the false doctrine spread broadcast today—that if the Lord does not do good to the sinner, he will at least not do him evil; therefore, men presume on his mercy and go forward in their sins, heaping up "wrath against the day of wrath and revelation of the righteous judgment of God; who will render to every man according to his deeds" (Rom. 2:5-6).

The argument that God is too good to punish men does not alter the matter. God is good, but his goodness is harmonious with his justice; and justice demands the execution of law against wrongdoers. "Behold therefore the goodness and severity of God: on them which fell, severity; but toward thee, goodness, if thou continue in his goodness: otherwise thou also shalt be cut off" (Rom. 11:22). The goodness of God is manifested specially toward those "who continue in his goodness." "The Lord is good, a stronghold in the day of trouble; and he knoweth them that trust in him" (Nah. 1:7).

Every verse of Psalm 136 contains the words "his mercy endureth forever"; but an examination shows that it is toward *his own people* that his mercy is everlasting. The same psalm shows that while God was manifesting his mercy toward Israel he at the same time "smote Egypt," "overthrew Pharaoh and his host in the Red Sea," and "smote great kings" in the wilderness. The love of God, therefore, demands the eternal separation of the wicked from the righteous—not love for the wicked, but love for his own people. He even threatened the wrongdoers in Israel: "I will punish you for all your iniquities" (Amos 3:2). Again he says, "I will punish the world for their evil, and the wicked for their iniquity" (Isa. 13:11).

While God is a God of love, it must be remembered that *love* is only one of his attributes. Justice is one of his attributes as truly as is love. Since God is a perfect being, we must expect to find in him the perfect and harmonious expression of all his attributes, and no manifestation of his attributes in any way reflects upon his character, but simply exhibits his character as it really is.

Degrees of Punishment

The Bible also teaches that there will be degrees of punishment. Paul says that in the day of judgment God will "render to every man according to his deeds" (Rom. 2:6). Men become doubly responsible by the light which they receive. Jesus says, "If I had not come and spoken unto them, they had not had sin: but now they have no cloak for their sin" (John 15:22). "That sin by the commandment might become exceeding sinful" (Rom. 7:13). Christ said to Pilate, "He that delivered me unto thee hath the greater sin" (John 19:11).

Since our sins are estimated in accordance with the light received, our punishment also will be regulated accordingly. For this reason Peter says concerning backsliders, "It had been better for them not to have known the way of righteousness, than, after they have known it, to turn from the holy commandment" (II Pet. 2:21). "For if we sin willfully after that we have received the knowledge of the truth, there remaineth no more sacrifice for sins. . . . Of how much sorer punishment, suppose ye, shall he be thought worthy, who hath trodden under foot the Son of God?" (Heb. 10:26, 29). The greater the light and knowledge possessed, the greater the responsibility. (See Matt. 11:20-24; 23:14.)

From the foregoing texts we see that men will be rewarded "according to their works," that some will receive a "sorer punishment" and "greater damnation" than others, and that it will be "more tolerable" for some people than it will be for others. But all these degrees will be in accordance with the light received and rejected.

Not Annihilation

It is a favorite theory with some that the wicked will simply be blotted out of existence at the day of judgment. But the scriptural facts just shown—that at the day of judgment the wicked will be rewarded "according to their works," that some will receive "greater damnation" and "sorer punishment" than others—utterly disprove that theory; for in the case of annihilation all would receive the same punishment.

There are a few texts of Scripture that speak of men in this world as passing away and being no more, which is very true of earthly things; but there is no New Testament text *referring to the state of men after the judgment* in which it is even hinted that men will come to an end and be no more.

Malachi 4:1 is brought forward as proving annihilation: "For, behold, the day cometh, that shall burn as an oven; and all the proud, yea, and all that do wickedly, shall be stubble: and the day that cometh shall burn them up, saith the Lord of hosts, that it shall leave them neither root nor branch." This day of burning, however, does not refer to the future state beyond the judgment at all, but was to meet its fulfillment in the day when "the Sun of righteousness shall arise with healing in his wings," which day was to be ushered in by the coming of Elijah (vss. 2-5). This Elijah was John the Baptist, as the following passages show: Luke 1:13-17; Matthew 11:13-14; 17:10-13.

The work of Christ in the gospel dispensation is represented as a work of fire. (See Mal. 3:1-6; Isa. 4:3-5; 9:5-7; 33:14; Matt. 3:10-11.)

The language of Malachi 4:1 is metaphorical. The fire is no more literal than the wicked people are stubble. Both fire and stubble are simply figures of speech, as are the fire, soap, gold, and silver of Malachi 3:2-3. None of them apply to the future state, as can easily be seen.

Future Punishment Will Be in Hell

"Fear him, which after he hath killed hath power to cast into hell; yea, I say unto you, Fear him" (Luke 12:5). "The wicked shall be turned into hell, and all the nations that forget God" (Ps. 9:17). From these texts we see that hell is a place. But it is also a *place of fire.* "The angels shall come forth, and sever the wicked from among the just, and shall cast them into the furnace of fire: there shall be wailing and gnashing of teeth" (Matt. 13:49-50).

The punishment of the wicked is represented not only as in "fire," but also as in "outer darkness" (Matt. 25:30). Literally speaking, these two are contrary to each other; hence, we do not suppose that the fire will be natural or literal fire. In all probability the expression is figurative, the same as the fire, stubble, and silver mentioned in Malachi 4:1; 3:2-3. But if fire is the symbol, how terrible the reality must be!

Yes, hell is a most terrible place—a prepared place. Prepared for whom? "Prepared for the devil and his angels" (Matt. 25:41). It was not made for man. Fallen angels and demons are held in reserve until the day of judgment, when they will be cast into it. "And the angels which kept not their first estate . . . he hath reserved in everlasting chains under darkness unto the judgment of the great day" (Jude 6). The demons know of their coming doom; therefore, those in the devil-possessed men cried out, "What have we to do with thee, Jesus, thou Son of God? art thou come hither to torment us before the time?" (Matt. 8:29). But while hell was not prepared for men, yet if men choose to serve the devil, they will share his fate, for "the wicked shall be turned into hell" (Ps. 9:17). "Depart from me, ye cursed, into everlasting fire, prepared for the devil and his angels" (Matt. 25:41). "How can ye escape the damnation of hell?" (23:33). Hell is an actual place; its punishment will be real.

Everlasting Punishment

I shall now proceed to bring forward the different expressions used in the Bible to describe the punishment of the wicked in hell, also the duration of that punishment. Some people think that most of these various expressions are only symbolic. But even so, their symbolic character in no wise lessens the force of their application. According to Paul, the things of paradise are of such an exalted character that it is "not possible for a man to utter" them in ordinary human language (II Cor. 12:4, margin); therefore, wherever the things of that future world are described they are of necessity symbolical, objects of this world chosen to represent them.

1. *"Everlasting punishment."* The Lord has reserved the "unjust unto the day of judgment to be punished" (II Pet. 2:9). They are worthy of a "sorer punishment" than death without mercy (Heb. 10:28-29). "These shall go away into everlasting punishment" (Matt. 25:46).

2. *Eternal "death."* "For the wages of sin is death" (Rom. 6:23). The death here mentioned is not that natural death which comes to good and bad alike, nor is it that spiritual death which is the direct result of sin, but it is an eternal state, for it is contrasted with eternal life. Natural death, as we have shown, is not the end of the soul's conscious existence, but is simply that state in which the human spirit is separated from the body. So also spiritual death is not the cessation of conscious existence, but is simply that state in this world in which the soul is separated from its normal condition of communion and fellowship with God. (See Ezek. 18:20; Isa. 59:1-2; I Tim. 5:6; Eph. 2:1; Col. 2:13; John 17:3.) In like manner the eternal death of the soul is not the end of its conscious existence (which would be contrary to all the other statements and symbols), but is simply its eternal separation from God. Natural death is something repulsive; men shrink from it and seek to evade it. It is chosen—with all its repulsiveness, with all its horrors—to represent that future state of separation from God—eternal death. "He that believeth on the Son hath everlasting life: and he that believeth not the Son shall not see life; but the wrath of God abideth on him" (John 3:36).

3. *Everlasting "darkness."* "God . . . delivered them into chains of darkness, to be reserved unto judgment" (II Pet. 2:4). According to the parable of Christ, the wicked "shall be cast out into outer darkness: there shall be weeping and gnashing of teeth" (Matt. 8:12). What a fearful thought! To be

placed in utter darkness is one of the worst punishments inflicted upon men in this world. A dungeon experience is generally sufficient to break the will of the most stubborn, rebellious criminal. Such is the figure of future punishment. How terrible, then, the reality must be! But this is not all. Instead of being an experience of short duration, as imprisonment in a dungeon, it will be forever. "To whom the mist of darkness is reserved forever" (II Pet. 2:17). "The blackness of darkness forever" (Jude 13). Is there not one ray of future hope for the wicked man? "When he dieth he shall carry nothing away. . . . He shall go to the generation of his fathers; they shall never see light" (Ps. 49:17, 19).

4. *"Eternal damnation."* "They that have done good, unto the resurrection of life; and they that have done evil, unto the resurrection of damnation" (John 5:29). "Ye shall receive the greater damnation" (Matt. 23:14). "Is in danger of eternal damnation" (Mark 3:29).

5. *"Everlasting destruction."* This word, as applied to the wicked signifies not the end of their conscious existence, but their utter misery and ruin. The word is thus used in the Bible over and over again. (For examples, see Exod. 10:7; Prov. 11:9; 18:7; Eccles. 7:16; Hos. 4:6; 13:9; Gal. 1:13.) "For when they shall say, Peace and safety; then sudden destruction cometh upon them . . . and they shall not escape" (I Thess. 5:3). "Whose end is destruction" (Phil. 3:19). All the sinner's plans and hopes, with his own noble self that God created for his own glory, are forever blighted and go down into everlasting misery and ruin—destruction. "Who shall be punished with everlasting destruction from the presence of the Lord, and from the glory of his power" (II Thess. 1:9). This everlasting destruction is not the end of conscious existence, but eternal banishment from the "presence of the Lord."

6. *"Everlasting fire."* "Shall be in danger of hell fire" (Matt. 5:22). It is "in flaming fire" that the Lord Jesus will be revealed from heaven against wrongdoers (II Thess. 1:7-9). It is called "a furnace of fire": "And shall cast them into a furnace of fire: there shall be wailing and gnashing of teeth" (Matt. 13:42); a "lake of fire": "But the fearful, and unbelieving, and the abominable, and murderers, and whore-

mongers, and sorcerers, and idolaters, and all liars, shall have their part in the lake which burneth with fire and brimstone" (Rev. 21:8), "And whosoever was not found written in the book of life was cast into the lake of fire" (20:15). It will be never ending: "Depart from me, ye cursed, into everlasting fire, prepared for the devil and his angels" (Matt. 25:41); "Are set forth for an example, suffering the vengeance of eternal fire" (Jude 7).

Reader, be not deceived by the false doctrines of men. Obey the Word of God and "flee from the wrath to come" (Matt. 3:7).

This Truth Forever Sealed

There is no way under heaven to evade the force of this multitude of Scripture passages describing the fearful fate of the ungodly. They apply to the wicked and to time beyond the judgment. If literal, the punishment they depict is terrible; if symbolic, it is worse. The language describes a future state of everlasting punishment—of conscious pain, suffering, torment, and wretchedness in hell. It either means what it says, or it does not. If it does not mean all this, then why do the Bible writers speak thus? and if they really intended to teach such a doctrine as this, what words, comparisons, and descriptions could they have employed to set it forth other than the very ones they did employ? Ponder well this question. They have well-nigh exhausted the language in this respect.

Notice, also, that the very same words that are employed to measure the endless duration of all that is good and holy are used to set forth the duration of the punishment of the wicked in hell. I will call attention briefly to some of these words and their use in the Bible.

1. *"Forever."* "The Lord shall endure forever" (Ps. 9:7). "The Lord shall reign forever" (146:10). "Forever, O Lord, thy word is settled in heaven" (119:89). "The word of our God shall stand forever" (Isa. 40:8).

Now let us look at the other side. "God shall likewise destroy thee forever" (Ps. 52:5). "If thou forsake him, he will cast thee off forever" (I Chron. 28:9). "To whom the mist of darkness is reserved forever" (II Pet. 2:17). "The blackness of darkness forever" (Jude 13). The very same word that measures the

The Destiny of the Wicked 187

duration of God's word, of Christ's reign, yea, of his very existence, is the word used to measure the time during which the wicked will be "cast off" and banished in "the blackness of darkness."

2. *"Forever and ever."* "The Lord shall reign forever and ever" (Exod. 15:18). The saints shall "possess the kingdom forever, even forever and ever" (Dan. 7:18). "Thy throne, O God, is forever and ever" (Heb. 1:8). The righteous shall shine "as the stars forever and ever" (Dan. 12:3).

Now turn to the other side: "And the smoke of their torment ascendeth up forever and ever" (Rev. 14:11). "Shall be tormented day and night forever and ever" (20:10). As long as the Lord himself shall reign and his throne in heaven stand, as long as the righteous shall "shine as the stars" in their heavenly home, just so long the wicked shall suffer the torments of hell—"forever and ever."

3. *"Everlasting."* "Everlasting God" (Isa. 40:28). "Everlasting Father" (9:6). "The righteous shall be in everlasting remembrance" (Ps. 112:6).

The other side: "Reserved in everlasting chains under darkness" (Jude 6). "Who shall be punished with everlasting destruction from the presence of the Lord, and from the glory of his power" (II Thess. 1:9). "Everlasting fire" (Matt. 18:8). "These shall go away into everlasting punishment" (25:46).

4. *"Eternal."* "Eternal God" (Deut. 33:27). "Unto the King eternal, immortal, invisible" (I Tim. 1:17). "Eternal salvation" (Heb. 5:9). "Eternal Spirit" (9:14). "The righteous into life eternal" (Matt. 25:46).

The other side: "Eternal judgment" (Heb. 6:2). "In danger of eternal damnation" (Mark 3:29). "Sodom and Gomorrah . . . are set forth for an example, suffering the vengeance of eternal fire" (Jude 7).

The very same words throughout that are used to measure the reign of the righteous in heaven, even the very continuation of God himself and heaven's throne, are used to describe the duration of the punishment of the wicked in hell. In Matthew 25, where the final reward of the righteous and the punishment of the wicked after the judgment are set forth, the same word is used for each in the same verse.

Chapter 26

OUR ETERNAL HOME

As children of the Most High, we are in the world, yet we are not of this world. As "strangers and pilgrims," we are simply "sojourning here" (I Pet. 2:11; 1:17). "Our citizenship is in heaven" (Phil. 3:20, ASV). For this reason we set our "affection on things above, not on things on the earth" (Col. 3:2). All our hopes, our desires, our aspirations, our longings are there.

This has ever been the conviction of all true saints here. The patriarchs of the old dispensation knew that their period of earthly existence was transitory; therefore, they "confessed that they were strangers and pilgrims on the earth." They were indeed seeking a country, but not an earthly one, for they desired "a better country, that is, an heavenly" (Heb. 11:13-16). We of the new dispensation share with them in the same future hope, "for here have we no continuing city, but we seek one to come" (13:14). Nor will this desire of God's people during the ages go unsatisfied, "for he hath prepared for them a city" (11:16). It is not to be found in this world, for all the promises of future blessedness point us away from earth to another country, a "better country," "an heavenly."

How inspiring this thought amid the trying scenes of life! When tossed by the billows of earthly woe, the soul cries out, "If in this life only we have hope in Christ, we are of all men most miserable" (I Cor. 15:19), but courage survives and faith brightens in view of "the hope which is laid up for you in heaven" (Col. 1:5). What "strong consolation" is this "hope set before us: which hope we have as an anchor of the soul, both sure and steadfast, and which entereth into that within the veil" (Heb. 6:18-19). When earthly reverses and losses come, we accept them joyfully, knowing in ourselves that we "have in heaven a better and an enduring substance" (10:34); for we have laid up for ourselves "treasures in heaven, where neither moth nor rust doth corrupt, and where thieves do not break through nor steal" (Matt. 6:20).

We are adjusted to every circumstance. When things go smoothly, we rejoice and give God the glory; when fiery trials are our portion, we rejoice also, inspired by the hope from above. "If ye be reproached for the name of Christ, happy are ye; for the spirit of glory and of God resteth upon you" (I Pet. 4:14). What does a little opposition or persecution amount to? "Rejoice, and be exceeding glad: for great is your reward in heaven: for so persecuted they the prophets which were before you" (Matt. 5:12). The eternal reward comes to those who endure to the end, for they shall have an abundant entrance "into the everlasting kingdom of our Lord and Savior Jesus Christ" (II Pet. 1:11).

A Sure Friend

Are we certain of this happy termination of earthly things? Yes, thank God! "For we know that if our earthly house of this tabernacle were dissolved, we have a building of God, an house not made with hands, eternal in the heavens" (II Cor. 5:1). "For the things which are seen are temporal; but the things which are not seen are eternal" (4:18).

We look not at the life which now is, but with eager joy and anticipation we press forward to that life which is to be. "We look for the Savior, the Lord Jesus Christ: who shall change our vile body, that it may be fashioned like unto his glorious body" (Phil. 3:20-21).

Worldly possessions, which are only "temporal," cannot hold our affections; we are "heirs of the kingdom which he hath promised to them that love him" (Jas. 2:5). We have "an inheritance incorruptible, and undefiled, and that fadeth not away, reserved in heaven" (I Pet. 1:4). Away with earthly attractions—Jesus and heaven are ours! The beauties of this world cannot charm our souls; we are citizens of another country, "a better country," "an heavenly." Scenes of heavenly beauty and glory have passed before our spiritual vision; celestial music has fallen upon our ears, and onward we press to that land of eternal rest.

When shall we enter this everlasting abode of the righteous?

"Let not your heart be troubled: ye believe in God, believe also in me. In my Father's house are many mansions: if it were not so I would have told you. I go to prepare a place for you. And if I go and prepare a place for you, I will come again, and receive you unto myself; that where I am, there ye may be also" (John 14:1-3). Where did Jesus go? "He was parted from them, and carried up into heaven" (Luke 24:51). When will he come again to receive us? "The Lord himself shall descend from heaven with a shout, with the voice of the archangel, and with the trump of God: and the dead in Christ shall rise first: then we which are alive and remain shall be caught up together with them in the clouds, to meet the Lord in the air: and so shall we ever be with the Lord" (I Thess. 4:16-17).

The plan and purpose of God have been complete in the mind of the omnipotent One from the beginning. Redemption itself has ever been present before him. Christ was a "Lamb slain from the foundation of the world" (Rev. 13:8); still, actual fulfillment did not take place until after the lapse of many centuries. The future and eternal home of the redeemed is but another part of the same great redemptory plan, and it, too, has been in the mind and purpose of God from the beginning; hence it is a "kingdom prepared for you from the foundation of the world" (Matt. 25:34); still, its actual preparation was a later accomplishment, for Jesus says, "I go to prepare a place for you and ... I will come again, and receive you unto myself." Then, and not until then, will the heavenly world be brought to view.

A New Heaven and a New Earth

This second coming is described by the Apostle Peter thus: "But the day of the Lord will come as a thief in the night; in the which the heavens shall pass away with a great noise, and the elements shall melt with fervent heat, the earth also and the works that are therein shall be burned up. Seeing then that all these things shall be dissolved, what manner of persons ought ye to be in all holy conversation and godliness, looking for and hastening unto the coming of the day of God, wherein the heavens being on fire shall be dissolved, and the elements shall melt with fervent heat? Nevertheless we, according to his promise, look for new heavens and a new earth, wherein dwelleth righteousness" (II Pet. 3:10-13).

This new heaven and new earth will be our future and eternal home. All the promises point forward to it. "Blessed are the meek: for they shall inherit the earth" (Matt. 5:5). The new earth is the earth that we shall inherit, for our "inheritance" is one that is "incorruptible, and undefiled, and that fadeth not away, reserved in heaven" (I Pet. 1:4).

The description given by the Revelator is still plainer: "And I saw a great white throne, and him that sat on it, from whose face the earth and the heaven fled away; and there was found no place for them. And I saw the dead, small and great, stand before God; and the books were opened: and another book was opened, which is the book of life: and the dead were judged out of those things which were written in the books, according to their works" (Rev. 20:11-12). "And I saw a new heaven and a new earth: for the first heaven and the first earth were passed away" (21:1).

The Golden City

This new heaven and new earth, brought to view after the passing of the present earth, will be the place of our future and eternal abode; "for here we have no continuing city, but we seek one to come" (Heb. 13:14). When this heavenly world was opened before the Apostle in apocalyptic vision he saw therein the eternal dwelling place of God's saints symbolized after the pattern of a great city, the "new Jerusalem" (Rev. 21). The actual elements that make up the paradise of God are of such an exalted and transcendent character that it is not possible for man to utter them in the ordinary language of earth (II Cor. 12:4, margin); therefore they must of necessity be represented symbolically, the symbols chosen being, of course, in their nature vastly inferior to the things thus foreshadowed.

What city is this laid out before us in splendor and magnificence? It is "the holy city, new Jerusalem," the city of "pure gold." Even its streets are of purest gold. It is surrounded by a "wall great and high," and twelve gates, each a solid pearl, give entrance. This wall is of jasper, built on foundations garnished with all manner of precious stones—jasper, sapphire, chalcedony, emerald, sardonyx, sardius, chrysolyte, beryl, topaz, chrysoprasus, jacinth, and amethyst. The glory of God itself illuminates this city continually. Here is "a pure river of water of life, clear as crystal, proceeding out of the throne of God and of the Lamb," and on each side of this beautiful stream stands the tree of life, rich in luscious fruits, and no cherubim with flaming swords are there to guard it. This is paradise restored. "There shall be no more curse." "Blessed are they that do his commandments, that they may have right to the tree of life, and may enter in through the gates into the city" (Rev. 22:14).

Our Home Eternal

This will be our eternal home. "There the wicked cease from troubling; and there the weary be at rest" (Job 3:17). There in the city of light we shall "shine as the brightness of the firmament"; yea, "they that turn many to righteousness" shall shine "as the stars forever and ever" (Dan. 12:3).

O bliss of heaven! Joy unspeakable! when we shall sit down with Abraham and Isaac and Jacob and all the prophets, in the kingdom of God, or shall gather with the ransomed around the great white throne, and there pour out our anthems of praise and thanksgiving unceasingly. O my soul, press onward! There is nothing in this world to hold thy affections. "Pleasures forevermore" beckon thee on to that land of excellent delights where comes no setting sun! My brethren, take courage! Thrones and dominions, glittering scepters and crowns of dazzling splendor are the symbols of our glory in the life that is to be. Heed not earth's sorrows. No sickness, no pain, no sorrow, and no death shall mar our happiness in the eternal paradise; for God himself shall wipe away all tears from our eyes. With time behind us, eternity before us, the angels and the redeemed of all ages around us—that will be heaven, our eternal home.